Design Thinking & Social Construction

A practical guide to innovation in research

Celiane Camargo-Borges
Sheila McNamee

B/S

Authors: **Celiane Camargo-Borges and Sheila McNamee**

Illustrator: **Lara Krenzinger**

Designer: **Tauana D'Ambrosi**

- - - - - - - - - - -

ISBN 978 90 6369 633 7

- - - - - - - - - - -

BIS Publishers
Borneostraat 80-A
1094 CP Amsterdam
The Netherlands
T +31 (0)20 515 02 30
bis@bispublishers.com
www.bispublishers.com

The Constructionist-Design Research Framework

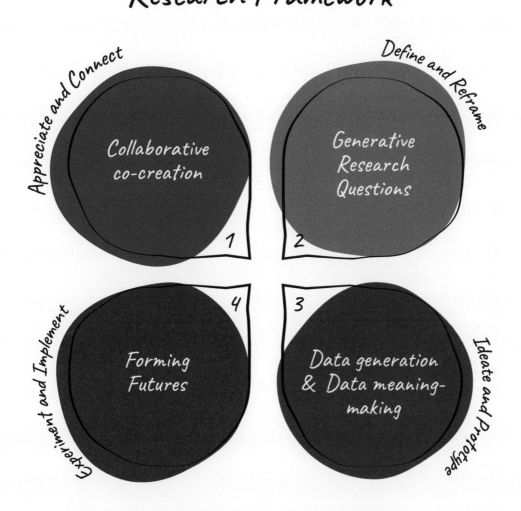

Appreciate and Connect

Define and Reframe

Collaborative co-creation

Generative Research Questions

1

2

4

3

Forming Futures

Data generation & Data meaning-making

Experiment and Implement

Ideate and Prototype

Unfolding new worlds

Content

Preface

Silva Jardim is one of my favorite places in Brasil, a location where I made friends over the past several years while bringing my Dutch students to work on their innovation projects. I am here, at the farm of friends, writing this Preface. The broad fronds of banana leaves and the lush vegetation bring cool shade to this one area of the Atlantic rain forest in Brasil's state of Rio de Janeiro. This area is not only filled with wild beauty and mystery but also hosts social movements for the restoration of the rain forest as well as community projects to produce organic food and cultural movements in an ongoing search for greater social equality. This is not only an idyllic place but an ideal space to bring this book to a close as well as my own sabbatical year traveling around South America, my home continent.

Throughout this year I have been immersed in multiple places and cultures and have been especially moved by – and have learned from – the traditional knowledge of local and indigenous peoples living in South America. I spent time with the Guaranis and Quilombolas in Brasil, the Quechuas and Aymaras in Peru, and the Tayrona, Kogi and Wiwa in Colombia. My travel and exposure to the diversity of peoples, cultures, and landscapes has made me appreciate the richness that we have around us and the great variety of ways of seeing and doing things. And this inspires — or should inspire — the need to celebrate diversity, embracing it for the new knowledge it brings to us all.

How can research tap into this diversity of knowledge and wisdom?

Along with my co-author, **Sheila McNamee**, we are committed to the movement of decolonizing research, embracing knowledge as a co-construction of all sorts of people in their interactions and not just belonging to an elite of academics. We want to inspire professionals to see that knowledge is not something only produced in laboratories or academic institutions. For those of us committed to a world that can be more just and inclusive, we must create space not merely to exploit it but to learn from it, to create with and to combine this plurality of wisdom into new possibilities for people and the world.

As I learned how the indigenous peoples often look at humanity and the natural world as one united whole instead of as separate and opposing dichotomies (nature versus civilization), I was inspired to incorporate those systemic and integral ideas in this book. The central theme of **Design Thinking and Social Construction: A Practical Guide to Innovation in Research** is to highlight the interconnectedness of ourselves and the ecosystem as we create knowledge. We show how nature, people, and our environments are related and shape our reality. And through the Constructionist-Design Research Framework, we explore how we can forge a new vision of what is possible as we participate together in the research process. We encourage researchers to become change agents, celebrating diversity, transcending dichotomies, and producing knowledge while also changing the system. We encourage researchers to embrace an ethic of constant learning and evolving, through a spirit of open-mindedness and by establishing mutually beneficial partnerships.

In this Research Framework we combine the philosophy of social construction with the attributes and principles of design thinking. We systematize the combination in this Framework that can serve as a practical guide for innovation in research. The Constructionist-Design Research Framework is a future-forming Framework, liberating the researcher from the constraints of so-called realism. It is a Framework that unfolds new worlds and fosters more promising futures through actively adapting with the systems of focus.

Lara Krenzinger joins this effort as the book's artist. Her illustrations translate ideas and concepts into creative and useful visuals, supporting readers to engage and learn in a practical, instructive, and active mode. **Tauana D'Ambrosi**, our designer, helped with the layout of the book. **Angelica van Dam** and **Andrew Gebhardt** read parts of the book, advising on content and form. We also would like to thank **Maria Clara Bianchini Borduque** and **Murilo Moscheta** for offering us their artistic eye and poetic sensibility.

We invite you, the reader, to join in this adventure, co-creating with us.

Celiane Camargo-Borges,
Silva Jardim, Rio de Janeiro, Brasil, June 2022

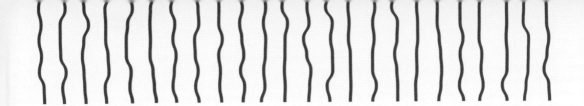

Introduction

Setting the Stage for a Creative and Innovative Approach to Research

Daily we are confronted with systemic challenges. Thanks to technological advances we can not avoid the rapid pace of social change, nor can we avoid the proliferation of diverse values, beliefs, and ways of being. Confronted with such diversity, it becomes impossible to avoid conflict – our own beliefs clash with other's beliefs. We often feel that our rights are more important than others' rights. In addition to the mounting challenge of clashing ideological perspectives, the institutions that have served as foundation for what counts as good, true, and real are also called into question, teetering on the precipice of obsolescence. The educational system, for example, is designed for a world that no longer exists. We face unprecedented challenges in the economy, grapple with issues related to climate change, sexual and gender identity, religious freedom, healthcare, poverty and more. With such a world in flux, how can we produce relevant knowledge that will assist us in coping with these challenges? How can research generate productive and relevant resources to create a thriving society? We believe that to address these critical issues, a new understanding of research – and a new way of engaging in research – is required. In a moment when technology, globalization, and concerns about shrinking resources are paramount, we need creative and innovative forms of research. Particularly as we acknowledge the mounting possibilities afforded us through technological advances, research – like technology – should be rooted in imaginative, inventive, and resourceful methods.

In this book, we offer a fresh perspective on research. Our approach does not look at the world and people as independent and separate units as traditional research does, but as an interconnected ecosystem. In this approach to research, we take relational processes as primary. That is, we believe that, in order to tackle the complex challenges we are facing, our modes of inquiry must focus on unfolding interactive processes (Gergen, 2021).

Our focus is on creativity and innovation as a fundamental part of the process of conducting research. Typically, we think of creativity and innovation as a "follow on" from research. That is, traditionally, research is viewed as making discoveries that then allow for creative and innovative applications (e.g., new pharmaceuticals, new efficiency rating protocols for the workplace, advanced teaching methods in schools, etc.). In this book, we propose a way of engaging in research that both introduces and reaches beyond new methods, embracing a fresh theoretical approach. Methodological innovation can generate new practices as well as new theoretical insights. We know that many research institutes champion tried and true methodologies thereby discouraging methodological innovation. However, the continuous replication of validated questionnaires, models, and templates – all ways of generating a standard way of doing research – reduces methodological pluralism. As a consequence, the generation of innovative processes that are more connected to our complex, contemporary world are limited.

In this book we combine the creative methodology and principles of design thinking with the theoretical relational approach of social construction. Through this combination, we offer a Framework that aims to be a practical guide for innovation in research. We believe that it is our job in this book, to show and support you in a creative research endeavor. We examine the central concepts of generative research and creative methods, demonstrating the "how." How can you innovate in the research process, thereby creating novel results and unfolding new worlds?

Chapter 1, Social Construction and Design Thinking: A Philosophical and a Practical Perspective on Research

This Chapter introduces the central features of social construction and design thinking showing how the integration offers a powerful mix for research.

Chapter 2, The Constructionist-Design Research Framework

This Chapter introduces research as a process of social construction using design thinking attributes and principles. We also introduce our Framework for innovative and creative research.

Chapter 3, Appreciate and Connect: Collaborative Co-creation in Research Phase 1

This Chapter outlines Phase 1 of our Framework by defining the appreciative stance in research and the appreciative researcher. We describe how to engage in processes of collaborative co-creation and offer some creative tools to be used in this Phase.

Chapter 4, Define and Reframe: Creating Generative Research Questions in Research Phase 2

This Chapter outlines Phase 2 of our Framework showing how to frame and reframe your ideas and how to make new interpretations and reinterpretations of information. We also describe how to create generative questions.

Chapter 5, Ideate and Prototype: Data generation & Data meaning-making in Research Phase 3

This Chapter introduces the methodology of the Framework. Here we describe how to gather data and make meaning. The researcher is presented as a change agent. We also describe how to design research with quality.

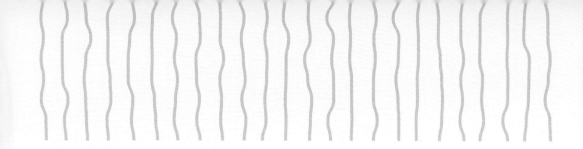

Chapter 6, Experiment and Implement: Forming Futures in Research Phase 4

Here we introduce the final phase of the Research Framework. We describe how to experiment with a prototype, creating a platform for collective creativity, relational responsibility, and imagination. We also provide some tools to evaluate your prototype in action.

Chapter 7, Research as Intervention: Transcending Dichotomies

This is the closing of the book where we describe the relevance of research as creative, engaging, and innovative. We discuss the importance of transcending dichotomies in research and the power of research as future-forming. The ethics of research is also covered in this Chapter. We end showing the powerful unity of social construction and design thinking and the core positions of a researcher in this Research Framework.

Social Construction and Design Thinking

A Philosophical and a Practical Perspective on Research

This chapter will introduce:

- Social construction and its central features
- Design thinking and its principles and attributes
- An integration of design thinking and social construction as a powerful mix for research

The Philosophical Perspective – Social Construction

Social construction is a movement within the social sciences that has developed over the past several decades as one of the most important and innovative paradigms of contemporary psychology (Burr, 2015). The focus of social construction is on meaning-making. Constructionists assume that meaning is created when people interact. Social construction also acknowledges that the meaning is never stable; it is constantly changing and is responsive to culture, history, and local situatedness. Social construction invites us to take a closer look at what people do together in local contexts since this is where knowledge (meaning) is produced. This means that, instead of searching for unified answers to the challenges of living, we start with an assumption that there are always diverse beliefs and values circulating in a culture, community, organization, or family. And, instead of attempting (through research) to discern which beliefs and values are the "right" ones, we engage in "curious inquiry" in an attempt to understand how diverse meanings are coherent for those who hold them. We center our interest on exploring the polyphony of voices and perspectives that play a role in shaping and framing the meaning of issues we confront in our families, our communities, our organizations, and our cultural institutions.

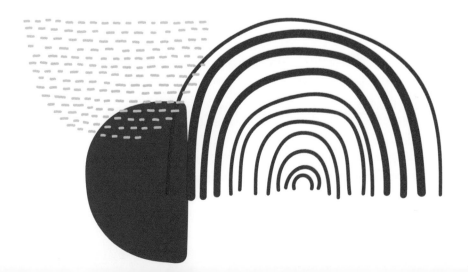

What is Social Construction?

Unlike traditional understandings that identify knowledge as the possession of individuals – inside a person's head – social construction proposes that all we take to be true, just, rational, and right emerges from relational processes (Gergen, 2015). In this way, we come to understand competing views of the world as emerging from very different relational processes – processes that are historically and culturally bound. The implications of this understanding are profound. Those with radically different values and beliefs – those whose knowledge of the world is foreign to us – are no longer wrong, irrational, or evil. Rather, what comes to be viewed as right or wrong achieves that very status only within a community of coordinated relations. For the constructionist, meanings are created in the coordination of people in their encounters with each other and their environment (McNamee, 2014).

We acknowledge the multiplicity of beliefs and values, the multitude of meanings that can be constructed for one object, event, or person. We are not proposing that "anything goes." We are simply trying to grant legitimacy – in local contexts – to alternative understandings. In order to do so, it is important to know how meaning (values, beliefs, realities) are created. As people coordinate their activities with others, patterns or rituals quickly emerge. These rituals generate a sense of standards and expectations that we use to assess our own and others' actions. Once these standards are in place, the generation of values and beliefs (a reality) is established. Thus, from the very simple process of coordinating our activities with each other, we develop entire belief systems, moralities, values, and worldviews. Of course, the starting point for analysis of any given reality is not restricted to our relational coordinations.

We can equally explore patterns of interaction or the sense of obligation (standards and expectations) that participants report in any given moment. We can also start with the emergent realities, themselves (dominant discourses as many would call them) and engage in a Foucauldian (1972) archeology of knowledge where we examine how certain beliefs, values, and practices originally emerge, which returns us to the simple coordinations of people and environments in specific historical, cultural, and local moments. The relational process of creating a worldview (reality) can be illustrated as follows (McNamee, 2014):

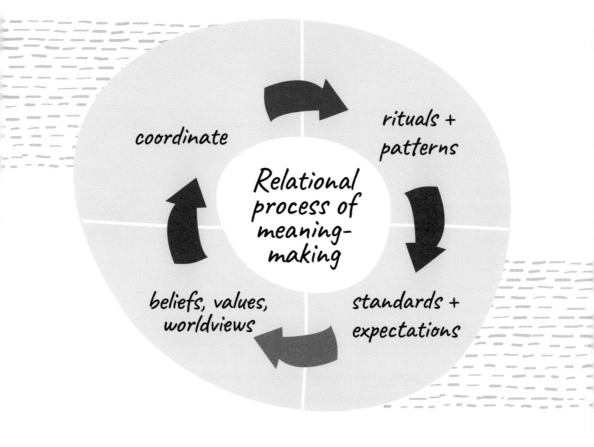

We create the worlds in which we live in our moment-to-moment engagements with others and with the environment. We also inherit previously negotiated ways of viewing the world. Yet, those inherited, taken-for-granted ways of talking and acting only remain so by virtue of our continued coordinations that serve to maintain what we take to be True or Real. In other words, what we do with others matters! We simultaneously live within negotiated worldviews and we maintain or change them by virtue of how we interact. For example, we presume that a visit to a medical doctor is "the right thing to do" when we feel ill. It is a discourse[1] (an unquestioned way of being) that has circulated culturally for some time.

However, if we failed to participate in this practice – if we prayed when we felt ill instead of visiting the doctor, and others did as well – the dominance of the medical worldview would cease. Thus, while we most often feel obligated to follow certain cultural and social practices, we neglect to recognize our own participation in keeping such practices alive (e.g., when we seek a doctor's diagnosis, we are participating in maintaining the dominance of medical discourse). Understanding the interdependence of our realities and our daily interactions clarifies how differences in meanings and entire worldviews are created and maintained.

We can note that, for those engaged in coordinated interactions that construct particular beliefs, those beliefs or realities are coherent and rational. Yet, for others whose daily interactions generate different meanings, thus different realities, the "other" constructions appear wrong and often evil or immoral. The next two figures illustrate two communities with diametrically opposing beliefs and values (realities), yet within each community there is coherence and rationality.

---

[1]A discourse is a way of talking and acting. For example, we can identify the discourse of science, the discourse of medicine, the discourse of dance. Often, discourses are ways of talking and acting that we simply take for granted as the "way the world is." Think about a visit to your doctor. She might explain what's wrong with you using a lot of medical terminology. For her, this discourse is just the "right" way of explaining your health. But to you, it very likely could sound like a foreign language that has no meaning for you. Paying attention to the various discourses circulating in your daily interactions alerts you to the multiplicity of both possibilities and meanings, values, and beliefs.

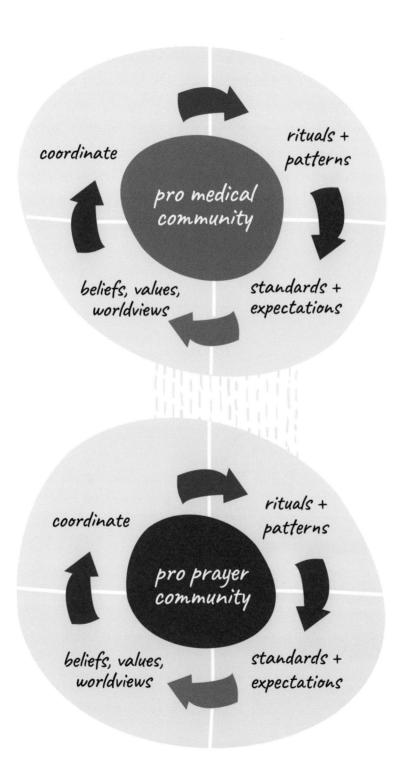

coordinate

rituals +
patterns

pro medical
community

beliefs, values,
worldviews

standards +
expectations

coordinate

rituals +
patterns

pro prayer
community

beliefs, values,
worldviews

standards +
expectations

While these differences are most often treated as a threat to one's own beliefs and values, understanding how a constructed belief emerges as coherent within a community, helps us to approach difference and diversity with curiosity and respect. Rather than attempting to judge which community is right and which is wrong, which is good and which is evil, we can attempt to understand how each community has come to construct their realities as they have. To do so requires that we put aside a desire for agreement or for a singular answer and, instead, adopt a desire to deepen our understanding of difference. In doing so, difference becomes less of a threat. It is no longer something to eliminate, but something to understand. Difference is the starting point – it invites our appreciation of the complexity of the social world.

In a nutshell, social construction asks us to:

assume diversity of beliefs and values rather than strive to uncover the singular answer

accept uncertainty and emergence rather than approach the world with certainty of knowledge

embrace complexity and interdependence rather than look at people and the world as independent and autonomous units

take joy in vulnerability rather than adopt a posture of self-assuredness

be open to innovative ways forward rather than ready-to-hand solutions

Central Features of Social Construction

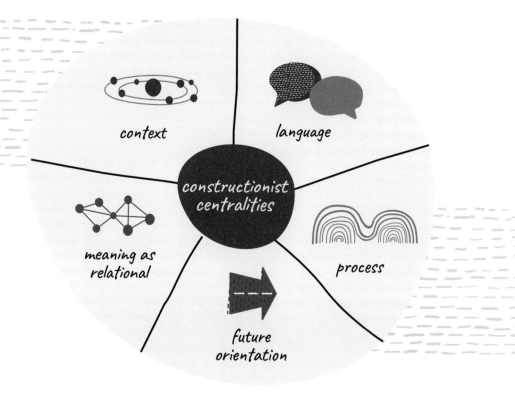

The Centrality of Language: Creating Local Realities

Constructionists are concerned with how meaning and understanding are created in interaction among people and in the environments in which they operate (Gergen, 2015). To this end, constructionists focus on language or what we refer to as language practices. Language in this sense encompasses much more than spoken or written words. Language includes all embodied activity; meaningful actions are always emerging within relational processes. The focus of analysis, therefore, is not the individual but is what people do together and what their "doing" makes. This calls attention to the relational and collaborative aspect of the theory – it is in relational processes with others and with our environment that we create, maintain, and change our social reality.

Given this focus on how local language practices create possible realities, constructionists adopt a critical stance toward taken-for-granted understandings of the world. Since interaction is always situated (locally, culturally, historically), it is reasonable to acknowledge the existence of diverse – and sometimes incompatible – realities. In other words, different communities, different cultures, and people living in different historical moments create different understandings of their world. With such multiplicity of views, the idea that we could uncover one Truth which would then allow us to predict and control our worlds, is placed in question. This idea will profoundly affect the way social constructionist research operates. We will see this later in the book.

By questioning what we take to be true, real, or good, social construction acknowledges the contingent nature of the social world. Many years ago, film director, Arthur Penn, offered a beautiful illustration of this point. He was talking about his film, Little Big Man starring Dustin Hoffman. In the story, Dustin Hoffman's character (a white man) is accepted into a Native American tribe. In fact, he is allowed to marry into the tribe. After a bloody battle leaving the tribe depleted of its male population, Hoffman's pregnant wife – a member of the tribe – asks him to engage in sexual encounters with her sisters in hope of impregnating them and thereby ensuring the continuation of the tribe. An action that would otherwise be considered immoral and certainly inappropriate to this community, is now transformed into a positive and necessary action. As Penn describes it, "As conditions change through (in this case) tragedy, we see that values, language, and morality change as well. It is the elasticity of meaning that is important to recognize and this, to us, is what social construction is about" (personal communication, May, 2001). We think that Arthur Penn has beautifully captured this relational appreciation for meaning. It shifts not simply to suit one's needs but rather cautiously and curiously to address the complexities of life. From a constructionist stance, we recognize that meaning – and therefore reality – is created in what people do together.

The Centrality of Process: Positioning Us in the Interactive Moment

Social construction focuses on processes in contrast to our common focus on end results or desired outcomes. It is important to note that this focus positions us in the interactive moment. What is happening between people is what becomes most important, and it is in unfolding processes of interaction that innovation emerges. Most often, we tend to orient ourselves toward a preferred result. For example, an organization might want to improve profit. That goal – increasing income – becomes the focus of attention. And, with that focus, organizational members challenge themselves to design methods to achieve their desired goal. The method to achieve the desired goal becomes formulaic (e.g., step A, B, and C), assuming that "the right" method will yield the proper results. Our belief that our methods are the right methods and will yield the right results render any potential opportunities that lie outside this linear approach invisible.

It is not so much the case that constructionists ignore desired goals, but rather the goals or hoped-for outcomes are "held in parentheses" or "held lightly." We say, "held lightly," because we acknowledge that the unfolding interaction (i.e., the process) might co-create more opportunities and will very likely expand possibilities for solving the matter. In other words, our focus on what people are doing together in the process and what the doing creates may very well construct goals or desired outcomes that differ from our original goals. Adopting this approach reminds us to "trust the process." Thus, we see that desired outcomes do not take center stage; they are noted and acknowledged. At the same time, there is no assumption made that the "right" method will lead to the "right" outcome. This is what we mean by the constructionist attention to process. Holding desired outcomes "lightly" allows us to be present to the moment and entertain many differing ways we might achieve our preferred outcomes and, importantly, how our preferred outcomes shift and transform by virtue of our attention to our unfolding process.

The Centrality of a Future-Orientation: Creating Alternatives for Desirable Futures - Constructing a Reality

Another distinction of social construction is the focus on the future. If you examine how we most often talk about social problems, you will note that a good portion of what we think we should be doing focuses on the past. We explore the history and evolution of a problem. When did the problem begin? How long has it been a difficulty? How have participants come to understand the problem? What do they think is the cause of competing beliefs about this problem? What have those involved done to try to solve this problem? The questions we ask direct our conversation to the past, as do the expectations of all participants (i.e., there is an assumption that, if we don't talk about what caused the problem, we'll never resolve it).

With such an emphasis on these past-oriented questions, we solidify the story of the past, making it "real" and indisputable. There is little room for imagining alternatives and creating the future. Probably more important is the logic that is embedded in this focus on the past, a causal logic, claiming that what went before always causes what follows. This logic limits the potential of creating alternative and more desirable futures.

We do not necessarily want to argue for a disconnection between past, present, and future. We simply want to raise the issue of narration. The past is always a story. And, from a constructionist orientation, we acknowledge that there are many ways to tell a story and many stories to be told. Others involved in the same "history" will very likely narrate it differently, taking different turns, highlighting different features, and demonizing or celebrating varied aspects depending on which perspective is taken.

A future-oriented approach can enhance the coordination of different world views. This is because we all understand that we do not yet know the future. We have not embodied it yet. And thus, to the extent that we engage with others in conversation about the future, we promote the relational construction of our worlds. That is, we invite ourselves and others into a moment of co-creation. We fabricate together the reality into which we might collectively enter. We call that co-creation in action!

This is not to suggest that talk of the past is wrong. We are proposing a collaborative creation of possibilities and one way to achieve this is with future-oriented discourse. In our talk of imagined futures, we invite coordination of many convergent and divergent understandings of the past and the present, co-creating together a variety of possible scenarios. Again, this form of relational engagement moves toward coordinated respect for multiplicity and difference. With this approach, our engagement with each other and our environments is always future-forming. This has strong implications for our Constructionist-Design Research Framework.

The Centrality of Meaning as Relational: Meaning is Not in the Head

It seems only natural to accept the idea that meaning is an individual's possession. After all, when we look at another person, we see a body that is separate from our own and others. We see eyes, hands, gestures, and even peculiar phrasings, intonations, and quirky movements that seem to belong to the person we are observing. Who would want to question if we have private thoughts, ideas, motivations, intentions, aspirations, emotions, and more? And isn't it the wide variation among our private motivations, intentions, ideas, and so forth that makes living so difficult? Aren't all the problems of the world, of social life, linked to the problem of meaning? Poor performance in school is a sign of a student's inability to grasp the correct meaning of the material. Social injustices, like prejudice, are easily explained as the byproducts of those who do not "understand" what is good and what is bad, what is right and what is wrong. The common belief is that genocide, economic instability, religious oppression, and political vitriol would cease to exist if we could control meaning.

The problem is that we cannot control meaning. And by locating meaning within individual heads, we contribute to the continuation of the problem. If only we could design the right therapeutic technique, we could eradicate depression. If we could create pedagogical practices that work for particular topics or types of people, we could educate the masses. If we had one tried and true research method, we could answer all the questions of the world. These hopes are heavily layered with that sense of rationality, logic, and linear thinking that we inherit from the scientific tradition. There is a method (i.e., the scientific method) that will lead us to truth – not only to truth but to truth with assurance.

When we assume that meaning resides within individuals, we gravitate to a world of experts – a world where others know "better," implying our own voices are inferior. This is manifest in the belief that, armed with the proper tools, education, healthcare, governing, and organizational endeavors can succeed. It proposes that years of experience on the part of professionals yield effective practices and correct assessments that allow us to efficiently answer questions such as, What is the most effective and efficient way to motivate workers? How can we eradicate disease? Which governing party will most benefit humanity? By embracing this individualist assumption that meaning is the possession of individual minds, we focus more on "things" (entities and objects) rather than on context, relations, and what people do together – in other words, unfolding interactive processes.

When we entertain a relational view of meaning, these premises take on a very different light. If we talk about meaning as a byproduct of our coordinations with others – our joint actions – then what is the job of the professional? What does professional training and expertise, from this relational orientation, offer? Social construction, with its relational focus, presents a challenge to traditional notions of expert knowledge and professional neutrality.

If meaning is constructed in the joint activities of persons in relation, then any theory or model is not a truth telling but is a local/cultural/historical way of understanding. It is local in that it is produced in relation to others in their immediate circumstances. It is cultural and historical in that it is produced in a specific place at a particular moment in time. Instead of a competitive quest for the truth, with the constructionist orientation, we are faced with the question of how to live together in a complex world inhabited by so many differing beliefs, truths, and values. The task at hand is one of coordination, and our curiosity is drawn, in this volume, to research as a site of coordinated meaning-making.

When we refigure meaning as relational, we regard it as a practice, a performance that inevitably involves more than one participant. This draws our attention to the process of meaning-making – as discussed above – as well as the context within which meaning is constructed. Our focus is centered on the multiple ways in which social transformation can take place. Further, our focus is centered on the participants engaged in the immediate moment and the wide array of both common and diverse voices, relations, communities, and experiences that each brings to the current context.

The Centrality of Context: Situational Sensitivity

In this volume we sketch the ways in which social construction offers a world view, a philosophical Framework, and a set of fluid resources for action that do not eliminate or demonize other traditions. Those of us who adopt social construction are not attempting to claim a preferred mode of life or to discover the best way for a person, a relationship, an organization, or a community to develop. Social construction, instead, urges us to attend to the traditions, the communities, the situated practices of the participants at hand – that is, to the local understandings – in identifying what becomes situationally valued.

To attend to traditions, communities, and situated practices requires a constant flexibility on the part of those involved. The purpose of social construction is to explore what sorts of social life become possible when one way of talking and acting is employed as opposed to another. The alternative that social construction offers is a relational one – one that views meaningful action as always emerging in context, within relational processes. If meaning is a byproduct of relational engagement (conversation, interaction), then we are free to pause and ask ourselves what other ways we might talk about this topic, this issue, or this problem. How else might we approach the dilemmas and conundrums we face? Research is about creating possibilities rather than uncovering truths.

The Practical Perspective – Design Thinking

Design thinking is our practical perspective in this book. It is a creative perspective with an array of tools and premises about collective creativity achieved through co-creation. In design thinking, there is an invitation to a contextual, interactive, and collaborative attitude. To us, social construction and design thinking are a good match. Especially if we are talking about reframing traditional research into future-forming research, which is research oriented toward creating more desirable futures, research that embraces the interconnectedness of the world. Social construction is our philosophical Framework in the research design, as described above. In this section, we present what we refer to as our practical perspective, offering certain attributes and a variety of active tools with which to work.

Design and Design Thinking

Design thinking evolved from the design discipline. Traditionally, a design approach has been concerned with creating new products or enhancing the look or the functionality of products as well as brand awareness (Kolko, 2015). However, the way designers work attracts the attention of other professionals. Specifically, a designer focuses on their clients (i.e., they are user-centered), experimenting throughout the design process to make sure the results are successful, always maintaining a sensitivity to the context in which their product will be implemented. Other disciplines began to embrace design methodology in an attempt to be innovative when creating their own products, services, and experiences. A design approach has been applied across sectors such as education, organization development, healthcare, government, and more. In design thinking, the focus is not simply on creating products but also – and especially – on designing human processes and human-centered activities for innovation, thereby generating open-ended possibilities for action as well as for collaborative work.

We can see design thinking growing in education (Gottlieb, Wagner, Wagner, & Chan, 2017; Melles, Howard, & Thompson-Whiteside, 2012; Lugmayr, 2011) and in business education to promote entrepreneurial capabilities (Bissola, Imperatori, & Biffi, 2017). However, we see much less applied in standard research. The book, Design Thinking Research: Making Design Foundational (Plattner, Meinel, & Leifer, 2016) claims that design thinking should become a foundational approach to science, especially in the areas of technology and innovation. The authors bring forward the tools and techniques that design thinking provides for enabling team collaboration in research; they also talk about a central factor in innovative research which is creativity and creative confidence. Finally, the authors propose the creation of a metric to measure creativity in organizations, thereby enabling information transfer and the sharing of experience and knowledge. While we are not claiming to make design thinking foundational, we are affirming the utility of design thinking in research. That utility centers on the way in which design thinking embraces creativity and innovation to form new futures. And, with that focus, we can see the affinity between social construction and design thinking.

What is Design Thinking?

Design thinking is one aspect of the design discipline. It has been growing as a creative and innovative way of working with various formats to tackle more complex problems (Kimbell, 2011). This angle of design thinking was initiated by scholars at Stanford University and was quickly adopted by IDEO, a design company that systematized the design methodology (Brown, 2009). IDEO's methodology is built around three steps: (1) inspiration: which is about understanding the context, the topic, and becoming inspired by opportunities, (2) ideation: which is about framing and reframing the topic in an attempt to emerge at the core of the issue thereby initiating a process of generating ideas, prototyping and testing, and (3) implementation: which is where the emergent ideas that have been prototyped and tested are implemented and put into practice (Brown & Wyatt 2010). IDEO's three steps comprise what is viewed as the classic design steps.

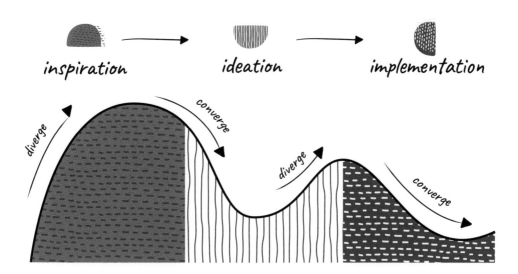

Many other authors have adapted, expanded, and re-created IDEO's methodology, maintaining the core ideas while offering other angles.

Imagineering Design Methodology

One example of an expanded IDEO methodology is the Imagineering Design Methodology (Nijs, 2019) which adds two Phases to each of the three steps identified in the IDEO methodology.

imagineering three steps	two phases in each step	description
Inspiration	A-ppreciating	This is about understanding the issue in an appreciative way, exploring the different elements that might play a role in a specific topic investigated.
	B-reathing	This is about taking a step back and a long breath before coming to conclusions about the various appreciative explorations offered. Based on all the material collected, this is about discovering generativity, as well as understanding the golden nuggets of the topic.
Ideation	C-reating	Here, the main actors are invited to interact and create a generative image or word that has the aim of reframing meanings and engaging in transformation, thereby creating a form of tension among diverse ideas.
	D-eveloping	Here the aim is to translate the generative image into tangible actions/proposals.
Implementation	E-nabling	This phase is about developing environments or platforms to enable engagement and commitment to the actions/proposals.
	F-lourishing	Here, the focus is on creating actions for sustainable flourishing.

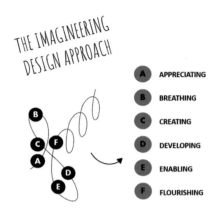

THE IMAGINEERING DESIGN APPROACH

A APPRECIATING

B BREATHING

C CREATING

D DEVELOPING

E ENABLING

F FLOURISHING

(Model developed by the Imagineering Masters Team)

The Imagineering methodology is a design approach focused on self-organizing life forms and the ways in which they interact with their environment (Banathy, 1996), centering on interdependence, non-linear, and open relations (Corning, 2012; Cross, 2006). With that understanding, Imagineering views organizations and society from a complex and interconnected perspective. The Imagineering design approach employs the idea of creating a generative image or a powerful word with the goal of provoking a creative tension that results in reframing meanings and bringing forth a new perspective about a topic or a system. The generative image or word from the C-reating Phase is the bridge between the actual reality and the future that is to be created. Thus, by having a generative image provoking a creative tension, new meanings can emerge, and new realities can be created.

ONE.WHY Design Framework

Another design approach inspired by the IDEO methodology can be seen in the ONE.WHY Design Framework, which follows the three steps of design thinking using different language: context design; human design; concept design. It also adds a "Why" in the center of the Framework to call attention to the purpose.

Context Design	Understand Discover Focus	This is about unraveling context. Instead of solving a challenge as given, the team will discover and focus on relevant issues. It will generate opportunities by exploring trends & technologies, discover new future scenarios, and determine the key stakeholders.
Human Design	Empathize Position Define	With a mindful and empathetic approach, this phase is about observing and engaging with people, immersing them in their experiences. In this way, needs, frictions, and insights will be identified, analysed, interpreted, and reframed into future scenarios.
Concept Design	Create Experiment Share	This is about iteratively generating ideas, new concepts, and business models. It uses nature for inspiration (biomimicry). Through prototypes, experiments, and position statements, new concepts and business models will be tested with real customers and end-users.

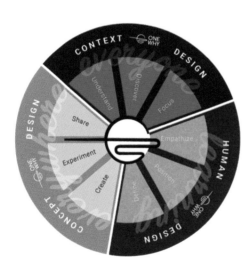

This Framework was created by Mariette Huizinga, the founder of ONE.WHY and it is used to innovate and create solutions in the education sector. The idea is that, in sharing different perspectives, you create an environment where everyone is learning. You invite a culture that encourages personal initiative, imagination, experimenting and acceptance of failure.

Despite the differences and diversity in the design Frameworks, they all work with the core principles of design thinking, focusing on bringing people together, expanding perspectives, and promoting connection and interaction for new creations. Design thinking offers a collection of tools and creative working formats that facilitate collaboration, engagement, and participation in a project (Rooijackers, Camargo-Borges, Marée, Weber & Brink, 2016). When these elements merge, innovation happens!

The attitude design thinkers embrace, together with the premises of collective creativity achieved through co-creation, provide the practical perspective of this book.

Design Thinking Centralities: Attitudes and Attributes

Design thinking creates and nurtures a human-centric approach to any issue (Luka, 2019). This means that design thinking is always focused on being inclusive and useful to the people involved. When participants experience the utility of what they are doing together, they become tuned in to the specific context and, consequently, the endeavor becomes connected and useful to the broader surroundings and sensitive to the conditions presented. Furthermore, design thinking fosters creativity through interdisciplinary alliances. It encourages collaboration across disciplinary boundaries to expand perspectives and innovate on a topic (Lindberg, Noweski, and Meinel, 2010). Design thinking also engages a diversity of participants in better understanding a topic and in raising a multiplicity of perspectives to co-create different possibilities. This inspires "an inquiry space where diverse views can be in dialogue with each other" (Alvesson and Deetz, 2000 in McNamee, 2010, pp. 16-17).

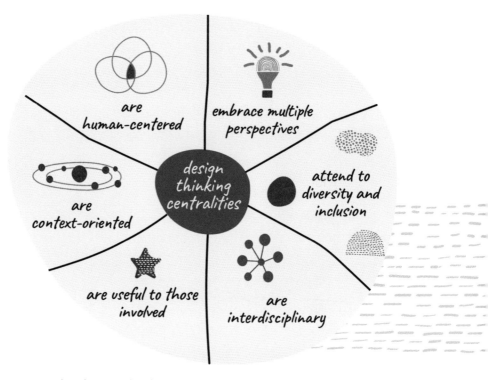

As we can see, the design thinking process is central to innovation. Creativity and playfulness are powerful elements that reframe a topic that has, to date, been seen in a singular way into multiple ideas to be prototyped, tested, and then implemented (Kimbell, 2011). With its collection of tools, design thinking offers creative working formats to design conversations and gather data, while encouraging participants to expand their own view on a topic and create new actions.

Because design thinking is focused on social change, innovation, and creativity, when connected to research, it contributes to the idea that research is a form of social intervention (McNamee, 1988). This is an important distinction because, traditionally and commonly, we see research as a process of discovery. Yet, research inspired by design thinking is a process of co-creation – together, participants actually generate their data. Design thinking research is an invitation to engage, to reflect, and consequently to create new forms of action. Research transforms social life, not because it "discovers" the Truth about some phenomenon but because it generates new ways of understanding and making meaning of the phenomenon.

Design Thinking and Social Construction Combined: A Powerful Mix for Research!

When adopting a design attitude within the social constructionist stance, we create a powerful mix for creativity and innovation in research.

In common, both favor:

More important, the articulation between design thinking and social construction strengthens both approaches. On one hand, design thinking gains a vocabulary that supports and offers theoretical legitimacy for research that embraces relationality, fluidity, and a future-orientation. On the other hand, social construction can be seen as a theory in action through design processes. In other words, we come to understand social construction as an ongoing resource for creating meaning in the social world.

Social construction can also bring theoretical support for the design processes that sometimes seem to occur just by accident or by miracle. Social construction can strengthen and provide a language for the importance of dialogue, co-creation, engagement, and participation in design processes. It shapes a space for interaction such that new meanings can be co-created thereby promoting transformation.

Transformative Concepts Connecting Social Construction & Design Thinking

Researcher-researched relations are no longer taken for granted as "the way things are" but are recognized as byproducts of particular ways of talking. We can talk of researchers "researching subjects" or we can talk of research as a collaboratively achieved activity where all involved are co-researchers.

Talk of individual knowledge or of mental operations gives way to an emphasis on relational processes – what people do together.

Relational processes construct both stability and change; they may close down or open up possible worlds.

Relational processes are viewed as interactions that maintain, deconstruct, or reconstruct local forms of life .

Creative processes are embraced in research to promote innovation.

The unitary conception of the person gives way to a dialogic, multiple self that is in ongoing construction .

In sum

In this Chapter we have set the stage for the remainder of the book by presenting conceptual ideas and practices of two approaches that, when combined, promote creativity and innovation in research. The proposal here is to embrace design thinking principles, attributes, attitude and tools, with the philosophy and central aspects of social construction. The constructionist approach to research emphasizes the co-creation of knowledge that is useful for those involved. Researchers and participants together create new forms of action thereby creating alternative possibilities for society, organizations, and communities. Design thinking is a practical Framework that provides actionable resources for the philosophical ideas of social construction. Together they become a powerful mix!

In the next Chapter we will introduce the Constructionist-Design Research Framework. Each subsequent Chapter walks through each Phase of the Framework and offers an illustration as a practical guide. We hope this illustration serves as a "how to" resource. The final Chapter connects all the Phases and shows how this Framework generates future-forming research. We invite you to consider a research approach that is less interested in focusing on "what is" and instead moves us towards "what might be" (Gergen, 2014).

Final questions for reflection and application to your project:

- Can you think of ways that design thinking and social construction can strengthen your research/project?

- Can you think of some central features of social construction that can be a resource for creating meaning in your work?

- What are the principles of design thinking that can foster creativity throughout the research process?

- Do you know/Can you recall other creative methodologies inspired by design thinking or Social Construction?

The Constructionist-Design Research Framework

This chapter will introduce:

- Research from a constructionist perspective
- Research as a process of social construction using designing research principles
- A framework for innovative and creative research

Introduction

In this Chapter we unfold our approach to research, describing it as a process of social construction. We explain how the blending of design thinking with social construction can enable creativity and innovation in inquiry. For that, we introduce designing-research principles and our Constructionist-Design Research Framework, displaying each Phase. We provide tangible explanations of this approach to promote more participatory forms of research, bringing innovation to the research process.

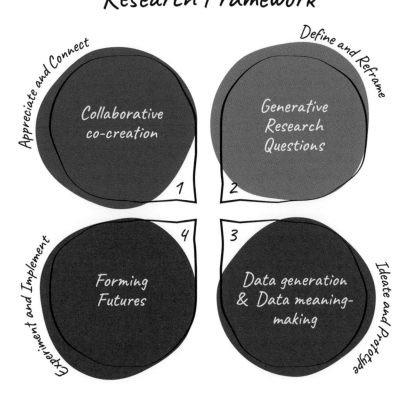

Constructionist-Design Research Framework

Appreciate and Connect

1. Collaborative co-creation

Define and Reframe

2. Generative Research Questions

Experiment and Implement

4. Forming Futures

3. Data generation & Data meaning-making

Ideate and Prototype

Unfolding new worlds

What is research?

As we are presenting a Framework on research, it is important to start with this fundamental question: What is research?

Research starts with curiosity...

... Curiosity about some aspect of our everyday life. We might be curious about effective leadership, about creating robust communities, or about how to create a vibrant classroom environment. Imagine a university professor who is eager to connect with students, who is excited to share with her learners the course material. In an attempt to gain an understanding of how to best engage her students, she can immerse herself in the voluminous literature on teaching effectiveness. But she could also open discussion – with her students – about what might excite them and maintain their engagement. The latter strategy focuses on co-action. Here the professor opens her exploration to those who will be most affected by her research on teaching effectiveness. We offer this small illustration to highlight the centrality of curiosity in the research process as well as the option to invite those who will be touched by our research into the very process itself.

In this book, we invite you to embrace your curiosity. Consider the issues that capture your attention. Once you have identified the topics, conundrums, and situations that pique your curiosity, we would like you to consider the relational processes – that is, the interactions – that appear to be central to your topic. As we pointed out in Chapter 1, the focus on relational processes is the hallmark of a constructionist orientation where there is a shift from examining objects (whether they be individuals, groups, organizations, or communities) to attending to what we refer to as language or language processes.

Research is about language processes

To the constructionist, language is not simply a tool or vehicle used to transmit or exchange information about the world. Rather, language is seen as constructing our worlds. What we do together actually makes our social worlds. This is an important distinction for many reasons but, in this context, this distinction is significant because it invites a reconstruction of our accepted view of research. Research here is embraced as a relational process that constructs our worlds; this is very different from the focus on discovering how the world is and seeking causal explanations.

Research constructs knowledge and possible worlds

Generally, research is associated with discovery. Those who engage in research with this attitude are immersed in a desire to discover the world "as it really is." According to Woolgar (1996), this is called the Received View of Science (RVS). The RVS postulates that the world is made up of independent entities that can be discovered, understood, or known through objective methods. The RVS assumes that if we ask the "right" questions, to the "right" people, in the "right" place and use the "right" tools to analyze the results of our research, we will discover a universal truth. For that it embraces neutrality, objectivity, replicability, and predictability as central components of any research process. These assumptions lead, in turn, to causal relationships in research, otherwise known as the logic of "if . . . then," generating a linear view of reality, typically disconnected from historical, cultural, and contextual features.

Yet, positioned within a constructionist view, we are examining the interactive, on-going, and unfolding processes of people in relation with each other and their environments. We are curious about what sorts of worlds particular forms of interaction – particular ways of talking and acting – make possible. When we construct knowledge, we construct our worlds.

If we embrace knowledge as co-created in contextual and historical relational processes, then research, as a relational process itself, opens us to the possibility of re-constructing forms of knowledge and ways of acting. This view recognizes research as "future-forming" (Gergen, 2014). We should note that most views of research are focused on uncovering what is already believed to exist – completely the opposite of viewing research as forming our futures. And, in forming the future, there is ample space for creativity and innovation through the acknowledgement that those participating in our research are co-constructing the research process with us. Consequently, research results become more user-centered and context-related, ultimately proposing future directions (Camargo-Borges, 2017; Camargo-Borges & Rasera, 2013).

This paradigm shift in research challenges the traditional notions of prediction and control, embracing a context-sensitive and human-centered approach. Social construction is one of the movements that promotes this shift by acknowledging that what we come to know about the world is a byproduct of our interactions. This approach forges new ways of engaging in research, opens space for alternative designs, focuses on locality and on generativity of knowledge and practice.

Recognizing that our knowledge of the world is constructed in social processes raises two important issues.

First, we are invited to view research in a way that differs from our taken-for-granted ways of understanding research.

Second, new ways of engaging in research are opened and thus knowledge production, itself, is reframed. Since constructionists give precedence to the constitutive nature of all inquiry, we are invited to explore what sorts of worlds we are generating, as well as what sorts of knowledge and understandings are being crafted, when we engage in any research process. In other words, our research interests, questions, and methods are neither neutral nor obvious.

Each is the result of a process of decision-making. And, it is important to note that our decisions flow from the assumptions, beliefs, and values that we hold.

Since different researchers/different communities harbor different assumptions, beliefs, and values, we can see that a claim that our research process is devoid of values is impossible. Rather than claim neutrality, we should ask whose values, whose assumptions, whose beliefs are being privileged in our choice of research topic, questions, and methods.

For the constructionist-designer, the "doing" of research can take many forms. And, each form of research that we adopt constructs diverse understandings of the world. Notice, we are not asking which form of research gives us the "right" results. Determining which is right and which is wrong (a modernist question) is replaced by which is most generative, and to whom? Which inquiry process will help us know "how to go on together" (Wittgenstein, 1953).

For constructionist researchers and practitioners, there is no way of talking about or conducting research that is off limits outside of any given community. This is not to suggest that "anything goes." There are standards and collaboratively crafted realities within communities (see Figure "relational process of meaning-making" Chapter 1, p. 23). Identifying these locally crafted realities as worldviews helps us recognize the ways in which standards and expectations bind a community together; one is not free to act in any way one chooses. However, the same standards and beliefs might very well be challenged within a different community. It is important to note that we all inhabit multiple discursive communities.

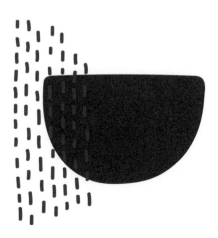

Research as a Process of Social Construction

Because the questions we ask and the methods we use have the ability to create new ways of looking at and understanding phenomena, we see research as transformative. As such, research is often aligned with issues of human rights, social justice, and a shift in how we view and design our organizations, communities, and our ways of living. It is about creating social change and improving human conditions in neighborhoods, communities, organizations, and societies. Research can be powerful and work against repression of minorities and is concerned with creating human flourishing, the creation of generative relationships, democratic communities, improved social conditions, societal welfare, and sustainable forms of life.

The attempts to create these changes require strong collaboration among multiple voices, needs, and interests. Therefore, as researchers, we must concern ourselves with bringing together diverse voices. For example, in relation to organizational learning, community development, or urban planning, how might we engage all stakeholders? Here, the ability to facilitate and engage in generative dialogue becomes crucial; a great deal depends on the researcher's ability to be responsive and to encourage people to engage in processes of learning and working together. Additionally, the surroundings and the current situation are of significant importance to the outcome and further progress of the research process.

Relational Research: Focus, Questions, Descriptions

A relational focus, as we define it, includes not only changed assumptions but also changed questions and interests. We shift from assuming we can uncover reality to assuming we are in the process of constructing a reality when we engage in research. This shift invites different questions and different interests. For example, instead of asking what causes poverty? we might ask how do members of this community understand poverty? A key issue concerns the kinds of realities that we are a part of and contribute to creating in our research. What sort of world do we invite each other into when we assume realities are community-based, local, historical, and cultural co-constructions? This stance avoids positioning the researcher as the expert and, instead, acknowledges that there are multiple and perhaps conflicting realms of expertise present in any research context.

The possibility to engage others in the research process broadens our resources for social life. Our emphasis is on the very practice of relational research as it opens up different possibilities, as a form of engagement that literally puts into action, and thus makes available, new relational resources.

Relational research features multiple forms of description (McNamee, 2010; McNamee & Hosking, 2012) where diversity can be explored as opposed to suppressed. Relational research creates a "thick description" (Ponterotto, 2006) that extends beyond observation of behavior to an understanding of research as a contextualized and situated practice that brings forward meaning and significance of the research focus (Geertz, 1973). Relational research is centered on results that "ring true" for research participants (e.g., clients in therapy or consultation, students in educational contexts, patients in health care services, community members seeking to promote local development) which means participants recognize the utility of certain ways of talking and acting. Constructionists are interested in the collaborative construction of research "results" among all stakeholders, co-creating ideas and practices that are relevant for their contexts. The challenge and the potential of social construction is its focus on coordinating the multiplicity of ways of being in— and speaking about—the world. In other words, how do we avoid selecting one way of being and speaking about the world and, instead, allow multiple ways of being and speaking to co-exist.

In viewing research as a relational process of collaboratively crafting meaning and understanding, we become mindful that all narratives are simultaneously descriptions of events and part of the event itself, due to the constructive nature of talk/interaction. The questions we ask are invitations to certain conversations and bring forth certain answers. That means we are constantly reinforcing realities and/or co-creating them.

We must ask questions such as:

In what ways is this research useful?

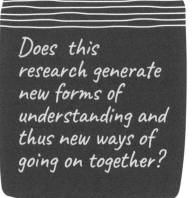

Does this research generate new forms of understanding and thus new ways of going on together?

What values are being granted authority?

Which political stances and relations are being muted by our questions?

And most important, we must remember that research itself is a practice – a form of professional practice, if you will. Thus, the researcher/practitioner divide is not a divide at all but a matter of stepping into diverse communities.

Research is a form of social change

Research, as we are elaborating in this volume, can be understood as a form of social change. Unlike research in the scientific laboratory where chemical compounds, for example, do not speak, the participants in our research are considered active co-researchers. As researchers (e.g., consultants, community developers, change agents, educators, etc.) we invite others to actively participate in co-exploration of a particular topic, situation, context, or phenomenon. It is therefore transformative.

It is important for us to remember that sometimes research is not initiated by the researcher; it might be community members, organizational members, students, or anyone with concern and commitment, who invites researchers to join in investigating a specific topic. Regardless of where the invitation is initiated, all involved are invited to offer their thoughts and opinions on the relevance of the topic. Embracing research as a process of social change can help us understand culture, people, places and spaces. It can also help us provoke change in culture, people, places, and spaces by engaging people in dialogue.

Research as a collaborative effort

Research, like any other social process, is a collaborative effort. The distinction between traditional notions of research and constructionist notions resides on a continuum. At one end of the continuum is the lone researcher or research team formulating hypotheses, designing methods and forms of analysis. On the other end of the continuum, we have researchers and participants working together to frame and execute the focus, design, method, and analysis of the research.

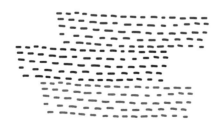

Traditional research   ## Participatory research

There is no doubt that, at both ends of the continuum, people are engaged in processes of constructing a world. Thus, to that end, all research is a form of social construction. But we must ask: What sort of world is being constructed? How much of a voice do stakeholders have in the research process? We acknowledge that all research is a process of social construction, and all research is relational. The issue is simply what sort of relationship one creates in the research process. Do we create relations which distance and objectify research participants (as in traditional research) or do we construct relations of collaborative, unfolding processes and social transformation (as in constructionist research)? The Constructionist-Design Research Framework we introduce in Chapter 3 embraces the latter of these two relations and could be considered "research from within" as opposed to "research about" (Shotter, 2011).

Designing Research Principles as a Process of Social Construction

Camargo-Borges (2018) and Bodiford and Camargo-Borges (2014) have explored combining design thinking fundamentals with a constructionist stance for innovative research. They have defined four core principles that can enable the development of a research project with a design-constructionist orientation, thereby supporting researchers with effective resources.

The first principle focuses on embracing research as **relational and collaborative,** holding relational processes as central; research is a collaborative journey. The invitation is to conduct research with others, and not for or about others. Participants are invited to bring their skills, knowledge, interests, experiences, and stories together to co-create the research/design process. As we engage in relational and collaborative endeavors, there is a move from the researcher/designer-as-expert to the researcher/designer-as-offering-expertise; this is a shift toward co-designers and co-participants of research.

The second principle positions research as **useful and generative,** centering on the utility and pragmatics of research. Focus is on how you engage in the investigation, aiming to create generative possibilities. As participants come together throughout the process, new understandings, new meanings, and new opportunities are co-created. Ultimately, the creative process produces meaningful solutions, appreciating each system as unique while also embracing future possibilities.

The third principle refers to the **organic and dynamic (or emergent)** aspect of inquiry. This principle emphasizes the act of conducting research as a fluid, dynamic, and continuous practice, allowing an unfolding as participants engage. While there is an emergent and organic nature to this way of thinking about research, this is not to say that there is no Framework to conduct the inquiry, since having an articulated purpose is important in collaborative inquiry. It is dynamic in the way that participatory practices are co-created throughout the entire process, involving researchers, participants, and theories. Collective engagement and openness are typical design methodologies and fully supported by the approach of social construction.

The fourth principle of designing research focuses on **engaging in complexity and multiplicity,** avoiding causal or dualistic positions. Embracing complexity and multiplicity expands our view to involve the whole system, appreciating the many different voices involved and welcoming other opinions and points of view to multiply new options and enhance plurality.

After unfolding our approach to research and offering the four principles of a designerly approach with a constructionist orientation to innovative research, we now present the Framework we are calling Constructionist-Design Research and describe how it can be used to design and conduct creative and innovative research processes.

The Constructionist-Design Research Framework: Unfolding New Worlds

We have developed this Framework to offer a research path to professionals/ researchers who are eager to innovate and co-create knowledge. The Framework supports researchers in organizing the research route. It can be used by any professional or researcher who has the desire to develop creative inquiry and to promote social change. In addition to offering a research route, the Constructionist-Design Research Framework offers a variety of resources to co-create meaning and action throughout the research process. The integration of design thinking and social construction provides a practical guide for creative and innovative research.

The Framework visualized in the image above proposes a path through four Phases. Each Phase has central ingredients of both design thinking and social construction to orient and position yourself as a researcher. Inspired by both orientations, the Framework is an unfolding process in which one Phase leads to the next one in a flexible way. Thus, the Phases do not need to be followed in a strict linear fashion; you can go back and forth if needed. The ordering of the Phases is simply a recommendation, based on our research experience using the framing of design thinking and on the philosophical stance of social construction. This Framework can support researchers in attending to important points in the unfolding process of conducting research; it assists in articulating what to do and how to do it, while simultaneously avoiding the fallacy that there is "one right way." It also calls attention to working formats that promote participation, co-creation, and emergence of preferable futures.

Below, we briefly describe the central aspect of each Phase. In subsequent Chapters we will dive into each Phase in more detail, bringing resources and illustrations to support your own constructionist-design research.

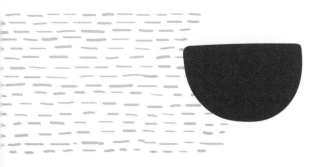

First Phase: Appreciate and Connect - Collaborative Co-Creation

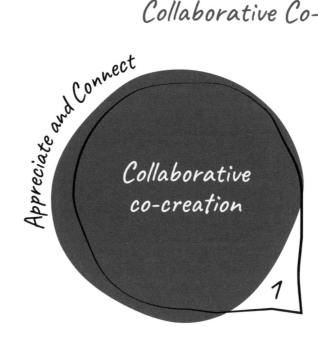

In order to initiate your research, you first need to understand your topic thoroughly. Understanding goes beyond facts and figures, embracing also experiences, values, and perspectives, especially of those involved with the topic. The first Phase of the Framework focuses on how to appreciatively enter the system in which the research will be conducted (e.g., the organization, community, etc.) and play around with your topic. We find a useful way to do this is to ask "what is" and "what might be." For example, suppose we are studying youth involvement in their community. We might begin by asking, "What currently is the status of youth involvement?" "What are the activities in which youth enjoy participating?" "How do other members of the community respond to youth involvement?" And, similarly, we might then shift to asking, "How might we increase youth involvement in the community?" "What has been most successful in attracting youth involvement in this community?" "How might other community members participate in our attempt to increase youth involvement?"

Acknowledging that any research process is a form of social intervention/ transformation, we are not (as is often presumed in more traditional research) simply promoting knowledge about a topic; we are also co-creating knowledge. Thus, as we frame questions and conversations, we are not simply grasping what is "already there" (i.e., the state of the art); we are already engaging ourselves in the process of co-creating new ways of looking at and understanding the topic. Knowledge here is not understood as something a researcher 'discovers' by virtue of her selection of the right phenomenon, formulation of the right questions, or use of the proper analytic tools. Rather, the way in which we frame a topic moves us toward an unfolding and newly constructed future. This brings an enormous responsibility since our aim is to expand, as much as possible, the understanding of our topic prior to creating our research frame. And that is why this first Phase is so important to the design of our research.

This suggests that, in our research efforts, we expand the investigation beyond a literature review. Reviews of literature are most often attempts to locate the "gap" in previous research. Rather than look for gaps (errors, mistakes, incomplete analyses), we embrace appreciation for the topic and connection with those involved. From there we can collaborate in co-creating the best framing for our research.

Appreciate and Connect – Design Thinking:

A designer always initiates a project from an appreciative stance, gaining inspiration about the topic/project from the people related to it. The designer attempts to understand and empathize in order to grasp as many of the elements involved and to embrace the varying perspectives on the topic by those connected to it (Camargo-Borges, 2019). In other words, we embrace here the competences of a designer and, unlike traditional research where the researcher presumes to understand and know how to approach and conduct his or her inquiry, the design thinking approach reminds us, as researchers, that others who are living in the context, who are connected to the research topic, have deep reservoirs of ideas, experiences, and questions. These ideas, experiences, and questions serve to "thicken" our understanding of our research topic. It assists us in defining what is central and helps in our framing of the unfolding research. The appreciative attitude comes from the

Appreciative Inquiry approach (Cooperrider & Whitney, 2005) which is based on the premise that language does not represent the world but creates it (Gergen, 2015). Language is fundamental to the creation of meaning. Meaning, in turn, creates action and action will create new realities (Gergen, 2015). Within this logic, a language of possibility generates a reality of possibilities, suggesting that everyday life is full of potential. On the other hand, a language of problems generates a reality that assumes everyday life is a problem to be solved. Therefore, it is critical that we pay attention to the language we use in framing our affirmative research topic. Following this appreciative stance, all participants' perspectives should be given voice. Using several creative design tools, we can examine well-established conventions and traditional assumptions in fresh ways. We can search for the generative core of the system to gain insights about the specific topic we are investigating. This will create sufficient input, allowing us to craft the next stages.

Collaborative Co-Creation – Social Construction:

To the constructionist, co-creation is the act of generating meaning and understanding. Words construct worlds. As we name, we create with others a particular reality. From a constructionist perspective, co-creation is both a concept and a practice (Camargo-Borges & Rasera, 2013). As a concept, co-construction relates to the constructionist epistemology that views people as relational beings. What this means is that we become someone as we engage with others within various environments. Who we are is not bound within us but emerges in the ongoing flow of daily interaction. We might think of ourselves as "professionals" but when purchasing our weekly groceries, we become a customer. In this way, our identity is both multiple and a byproduct of our interactions in the world. When we talk about co-creation as a practice, we are focusing on the creative process that can be designed and facilitated to produce new and alternative meanings.

For this first Phase of the research, we embrace co-creation as both a concept and a practice. As a concept, we understand that meaning is fluid and constantly changing. We understand that there is no right frame for a topic but rather, a decision that is made based on the context and the contributions from participants. As a practice, we invite research participants to co-create what is relevant and useful for the research. In Chapter 3 we will describe more about appreciation, language, and co-creation as practice and how to engage these practices in the first Phase of the research.

The goal of this first Phase is to gain an understanding of the existing situation of the research context and create a connection as well as engagement with all who are involved. Creating this connection and engagement is an important step for a participatory system and provides diverse understandings about your topic, thereby generating more possibilities. As we close this Phase of the Constructionist-Design Research Framework, we carry forward some insights to be used in the next Phases. In Chapter 3 we will present a number of creative resources that will help you gain more information in this Phase, thereby assisting in framing your research goals and questions, as well as defining the next Phases of the research process.

Second Phase: Define and Reframe – Generative Research Questions

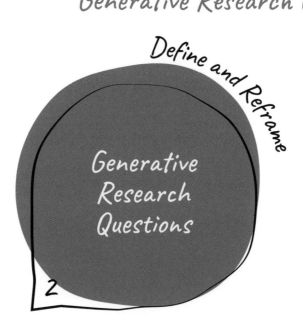

This second Phase is about framing and reframing the emergent results of the first Phase. The aim is to create generative research questions that will orient the research. The first Phase is designed to assist you in gaining a deeper understanding of the topic by becoming inspired, connecting with the context, and co-creating with the people involved. It is in this first Phase that what is crucial and generative emerges. Here you will see the potential, the energy of the topic. Now, in this second Phase of the Framework, you are positioned to develop research questions that will frame the inquiry process.

In this second Phase it is important to look at all information generated and start exploring different combinations of voices and perspectives that you have gathered in the first Phase. The varying combinations you develop in this Phase serve as different ways of framing and reframing your topic. By exploring various frames, you can develop a more nuanced and detailed understanding of your topic which will assist you in reframing your initial questions into well informed, generative research questions.

Define and Reframe – Design Thinking:

In design thinking, defining and reframing is the beginning of the ideation Phase where all the information from the first Phase is reframed into a central concept that guides the direction toward the design of products and services, the creation of spaces and experiences. In design thinking, a high concept has the power to concentrate all important elements into one word or sentence or sometimes a visual that creates an image of the project. What design thinking refers to as a "high concept," we identify as our research questions, as these will become the concentration of all the elements that need to be investigated. Our research questions serve as our guiding star for data generation, data meaning-making, and, at the end of the research process, decisions about experimentation and implementation (prototyping).

Generative questions – Social Construction:

The production of knowledge within a constructionist perspective is characterized by processes of deconstruction and reconstruction, resulting in what is called "generative theory" (Gergen 1994; 1978). Generative theory is theory that creates new possibilities, that ignites social transformation. It can be contrasted to a traditional image of theory where it is assumed that a theory tells us how the world really is (i.e., a process of discovery). In this way, we could say that the traditional notion of theory looks "backward," where the notion of generative theory is forward-looking, potential-looking.

Generativity and generative questions are approaches to knowledge development that have the ability to broaden the taken-for-granted beliefs and behaviors of the local culture, opening up the potential for dialogue, courses of action, and social change. Knowledge has its roots in shared interactions with others, gained through exchanges, relationships, and dialogue (Gergen & Gergen, 2004). Questions have the generative capacity to enact new understanding, directions, practices, and behaviors. Thus, generative research questions promote more creative and productive directions for the research process as "All questions are the frame into which the answers fall. By changing the frame, you can dramatically change the range of possible solutions" (Seelig, 2013, n.p). With this quote, we realize that generative research questions invite more openings for richness in our data. They have the potential to create more productive paths.

The second Phase of the Constructionist-Design Research Framework ends with generative research questions and a brief summary of directions to be taken (preparing the methodology: how data will be collected and analyzed). In this context of research, a strong generative research question becomes the "high concept" of the project, opening a vision for the research in the sense that you can now move forward with methodological choices.

Chapter 4 will offer more details about this Phase.

Third Phase: Ideate and Prototype –
Data Generation and Data Meaning-Making

Now, equipped with strong, generative research questions, we start the third Phase of the constructionist-design research process: data generation and data meaning-making. Up to this point, participants have been fully involved in defining the main goal of the project and articulating the research questions. We are now ready to engage in data generation.

Data generation is also seen as a collaborative process. Researcher and research participants – together, in dialogue – entertain ideas and understandings that can be combined, created, and re-created. In design research with a constructionist flavor, data is not seen as the outcome of using the right method to discover a reality; there is no assumption that there are facts waiting to be revealed. Data here is understood as data generation in the sense that meaning is always in motion; you are always producing meaning with others. The right method is always in relation to the context and topic researched. The same is the case for the difference between data analysis and data meaning-making. The interpretation of data (meaning-making) is an emergent process, bound and guided by the research questions. It is not the discovery of something that is already there waiting for the research to reveal. Chapter 5 is dedicated to this Phase. We will talk further about methodology and the difference between data collection/data generation and data analysis/data meaning-making.

Ideate and prototype – Design Thinking:

In design thinking, creative sessions are collaborative and take the form of participatory working formats designed to provoke new ideas and meanings within a project. They are often used to elicit "out of the box" ideas. In our research context, we embrace creative sessions to engage all research participants in dialogue. Using the materials found in the first Phases of the design process, participants are invited to imagine multiple futures and to connect with their personal stories and the context of the research.

Data Generation and Data meaning-making – Social Construction:

From the constructionist perspective, meaning does not exist apart from coordinated interaction with others (and the environment) or through what we call co-action. Meaning comes to life through ongoing interactive processes. One's words or actions alone are without meaning until another responds. For example, I can tell you, "I'm sorry." Yet, if you fail to respond to my comment, my "apology" has not been achieved; together we have failed to construct an "apology." If, on the other hand, you respond to me by saying, "I will never forgive you!" again, we have failed to give meaning to my words as an apology. It is only when you respond by accepting my words as an apology that this meaning is accomplished. It is also important to note here that my "intention" of apologizing actually has little bearing on the resulting meaning of my actions because I am (as you are) dependent upon you (and you upon me) to respond in a way that grants that meaning to my words.

Taking this concept of co-action into the context of research, we can say that data also needs co-action to be recognized as meaningful. We need each other in order to make meaning. Participants must collaborate in their understanding of what counts as data. In this Phase we create processes of coordination through creative sessions in order to generate meaningful data. Creative sessions can include many possibilities, such as mobile interviewing, cultural probes, locality mapping, etc (more in Chapter 5). Dialogue is also used here. Dialogue, which is a constructionist practice, is always organized to stimulate the creativity and imagination of the group, engaging with ideas in more complex ways leading to new insights. (We will discuss in more detail the notion of dialogue and its centrality to constructionist practice in Chapter 5.) In effect, social construction invites careful deliberation on the ways in which the generative potential of dialogue can be affected by the framing of the inquiry (Camargo-Borges, 2019).

After generating data, meaning-making of that data follows. This is the moment when all insights generated through dialogues promoted by the creative sessions are interpreted. The new meanings that emerge in this Phase are then framed into possible solutions, changes, or the specific goal of the research-project. In design thinking we call this a prototype. A prototype in design thinking is the creation of a draft version – based on the findings – of a possible action, product, or service. A prototype allows a quick 'trying out' of the findings, ideas, and meanings created. A prototype gives us the opportunity to collect feedback on what we have created. Fully equipped with that feedback, we are ready for the fourth and final Phase.

Some data generation and meaning-making resources will be offered in Chapter 5 to support successful dialogue and data interpretation.

Fourth Phase: Experiment and Implement – Unfolding New Worlds

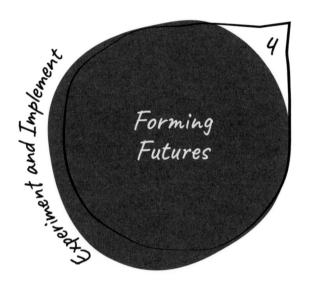

In this final Phase, the researcher is ready for the experimentation of the prototype created in the third Phase and for further implementation of the new ideas that have emerged from data generation and data meaning-making. The hope is that by experimenting and implementing these first ideas, you and the community involved in the research can better evaluate the ideas in practice, taking stock of what is missing and what has the potential to work well on a larger scale.

Experiment and Implement – Design Thinking:

Implementation is the Phase focused on refining the prototype to improve upon it. The prototype permits you to experiment, on a smaller scale, with what could possibly be a solution before investing larger amounts of resources (time and money). Prototypes help with thinking about solutions in a more experimental way, always focusing on tangibility rather than abstraction. Designers talk about failing quickly and cheaply. By experimenting, you learn rapidly about what does not work, spending less time and money on an idea that eventually turns out to be less useful. A quote from Tim Brown (2009, p. 105) on prototypes:

"They slow us down to speed us up. By taking the time to prototype our ideas, we avoid costly mistakes such as becoming too complex too early and sticking with a weak idea for too long."

This approach of design thinking can benefit a research project where, most often, the focus is on abstract ideas and knowledge at the expense of practicality. Attention must be given to what might be useful to the context and to the people. By experimenting with those involved, you can quickly understand what works and what does not.

Forming Futures – Social Construction:

To enhance the chances of a successful implementation of action/products/ services, it is important that the researcher and research participants come together to discuss the findings. This presents another opportunity to build connection and engagement among those involved with the topic and the context — creating relational responsibility for what is being created. Relational responsibility is a constructionist concept that emphasizes attentiveness to the process of relating, itself, as opposed to individual responsibility where the focus is on what any given individual does or does not do (McNamee & Gergen, 1999). When we are relationally responsible, we acknowledge our participation in what is unfolding; we embrace the project as a collective project in which everyone is involved. This is fundamental for a successful implementation and sustainable futures.

By understanding knowledge as a collaborative process of construction and embracing relational responsibility, the experimentation Phase is already forming futures and unfolding new worlds. By working on activating the findings and engaging those involved, you are already envisioning and building new preferable futures.

Experimenting with the Prototype:

To enhance your prototype and solutions you need to connect to all previous stages and put all the elements together. Experimenting with your final ideas for action/products/service, along with your research participants, promotes new insights and the creation of a space, also called the engagement platform.

Chapter 6 will discuss this further and offer resources to experiment with the research participants as you collaborate around the prototype, envisioning new, unfolding worlds.

Closing the cycle

With these four Phases, we close the cycle of the Constructionist-Design Research Framework, calling attention to the potential of designing new worlds, new opportunities, always embracing research as future-forming.

In this Framework we focus on the complex relational achievement, which is required to construct change and new directions. Different relational (research) processes – involving different persons in different environments – construct different realities (knowledge). This Framework enables these contextual, relational processes in a research environment. The Framework produces data as the result of an organic and dynamic process, generated in collaboration and participation with people in a specific context. In this sense, there is no right or wrong and the truths are always contextual, co-created in a specific time and useful to a specific environment.

In the Chapters that follow, we will explain in detail each Phase, offering resources to support you in developing your research. We will also offer illustrations from research projects.

Phases of the Constructionist-Design Research Framework

The Constructionist-Design Research in Action

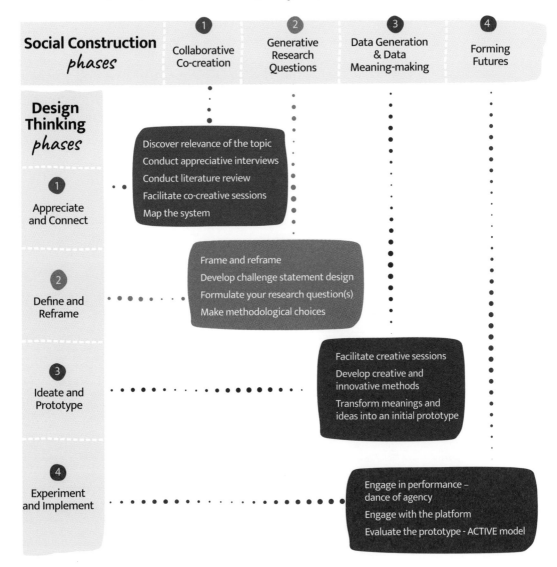

Social Construction *phases*

1. Collaborative Co-creation
2. Generative Research Questions
3. Data Generation & Data Meaning-making
4. Forming Futures

Design Thinking *phases*

1 Appreciate and Connect
- Discover relevance of the topic
- Conduct appreciative interviews
- Conduct literature review
- Facilitate co-creative sessions
- Map the system

2 Define and Reframe
- Frame and reframe
- Develop challenge statement design
- Formulate your research question(s)
- Make methodological choices

3 Ideate and Prototype
- Facilitate creative sessions
- Develop creative and innovative methods
- Transform meanings and ideas into an initial prototype

4 Experiment and Implement
- Engage in performance – dance of agency
- Engage with the platform
- Evaluate the prototype - ACTIVE model

Final questions for reflection and application to your project:

- After reading this Chapter, can you identify new ways of thinking about and approaching research and the creation of knowledge?
- How does the Constructionist-Design Research Framework support your project?
- How could you create innovative and creative research?

Appreciate and Connect
Collaborative Co-creation
in Research Phase 1

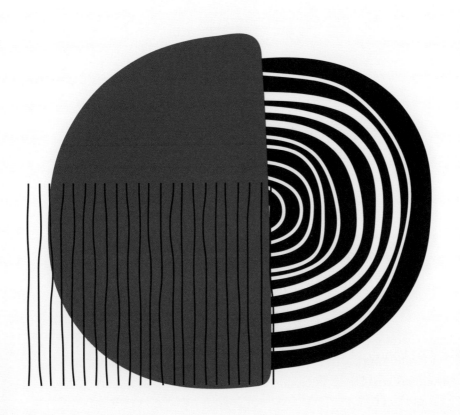

This chapter will introduce:

- The appreciative stance in research
- The appreciative researcher
- How to engage in processes of collaborative co-creation
- Creative tools for understanding and connecting with your research topic

Introduction

The Constructionist-Design Research process begins with appreciating and connecting with your topic. This is the first design Phase of the inquiry. When initiating research, you first must understand what your subject entails which means understanding the existing situation of the system with which you are working. The insights that you collect at this point will unfold in the next Phases by engaging in a process of collaborative co-creation with participants, as explained below. Equipped with the practices of design thinking and the constructionist epistemology, the aim is to reach beyond facts and figures by expanding your understanding of "what is the case" in relation to your topic.

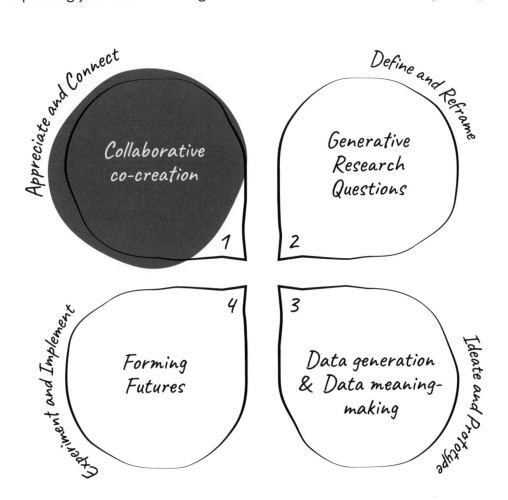

Appreciating and Connecting (with your topic and the system with which you are working)

As a Constructionist-Design researcher, you enter the research process with an appreciative attitude, allowing the topic to inspire you. You take note of what is going on and empathize with your discoveries as you enter the field. You take into consideration traditional assumptions of "what is" with an appreciative eye. In doing so, you are able to understand "what is" in fresh ways. For example, if you are working with a community that is concerned about issues of leadership, you might wonder if the idea that "leaders know best" might be a traditional assumption about leadership. Rather than eschew this assumption, an appreciation of it (i.e., "sometimes leaders might know best") could allow you to adopt a respectful stance toward community members while simultaneously opening space for alternative views of leadership.

With this new understanding, you collaboratively co-create with the involved actors "what else this situation/topic could be." Here, you develop a more complex understanding of the topic. Doing so requires using several creative-design tools to understand the system with which you are involved. These new understandings will be central in crafting the next stages of your project.

The appreciative attitude comes from the Appreciative Inquiry approach. Whitney and Trosten-Bloom (2010) describe appreciative inquiry as "the study of what gives life to human systems when they function at their best" (p.1). This strengths-based approach focuses on assets, capabilities, and resources of organizations, communities, and people – all of which can be leveraged and encouraged (Cooperrider & Whitney, 2005).

Appreciative inquiry is based on the theory of social construction, acknowledging that language does not represent the world but creates it (Gergen, 2015). Thus, if our interactions are marked by "problem talk," we construct and live within a problem-saturated reality. If, on the other hand, we talk and engage around what gives us life, what inspires us and share stories of high points, we construct and live within a reality marked by possibilities. According to Gergen (2004), meaning arises from what people do together and not from an individual's mind. Language and action create new realities (Gergen, 2015).

The way we talk when we interact with others, the way we choose our words and how we relate create connections as you initiate your research. According to the constructionist approach, we always move in the direction of that upon which we choose to focus, so we begin our research process with this in mind.

Empathy goes with appreciating

Empathy is receiving increased attention in the social sciences and particularly in this approach to research. Empathy is the effort or openness to understand the perspectives and experiences of others. It emphasizes interpersonal relationships and it calls attention to cross-cultural contexts. When we adopt an empathic stance toward research, we consider different perspectives, different ways of communicating and collaborating. We consider how we might establish shared goals and interests.

We could also say that empathy is another way of talking about the respectful stance one adopts when being dialogic. To be in dialogue requires that we hold the tension between our own views and those of the other. To achieve this, we position ourselves as curious (as opposed to judgmental) about the other's views and assume those views are coherent and rational within the other's lived experience. Adopting this dialogic (empathic) stance does not mean that we give up our own view, nor do we necessarily sanction the other's view. Rather, we respectfully, and with genuine curiosity, interact with the aim of collaboratively achieving new understandings.

The appreciative researcher

We find that an appreciative attitude helps the researcher (and participants) connect with their topic. This connection, in turn, assists in envisioning what and who should be involved in the project. Taking note of how you (and others) connect to your topic and being attentive to the potential implications of your connections will guide the direction of your research process.

Please note that it is not only an appreciative stance that assists in defining the contours of the research project. It is also important to gather multiple perspectives and understandings from those who are also connected to the context, issue, question, etc. In so doing, we start with an appreciative and complex understanding and avoid problematizing and simplifying. When we simplify the focus of our research, we miss the multiple ways that people give meaning to the phenomenon. Thus, by engaging with those involved – whether through interviews, dialogues, focus groups, or other means of connecting – we begin to co-create new ways of understanding the phenomenon and initiate our path toward refining the topic of the research.

How, exactly, can we start this process? There are many ways and here we offer one possible path.

 1. Play around with your ideas

 2. Start your literature review

 3. Field research and initial interviews

Step 1. Play around with your initial ideas:

Take a piece of paper and start organizing your ideas before expanding them.

Step 2. Start your literature review:

Once you have defined your topic and understand what you want to know about it and why, as well as its relevance, you must attempt to understand the context of your research. Are you operating within an organization, a community, a healthcare center, a school, etc? Dig into the system by asking questions such as:

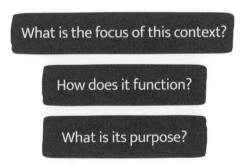

Then expand from the here and now context and describe what is beyond that, looking at how this topic plays a role in different places. It is at this stage that conducting a review of relevant literature is needed. What has been written about this topic/context by scholars and/or practitioners? What research has already been conducted and where is it published? What has been published about the macro-context? Some people refer to this as "desk research" in an attempt to distinguish it from action research where the focus is very much like the initial Phase described above – where the aim is to connect with those involved and gather their ideas and opinions. Here, on the other hand, we are concerned with exploring the already existing literature that describes other explorations into your topic and context.

To find publications on your topic, choose key terms that represent your field of study and search for them online or at a library. By reading the literature you can gain a better understanding of what has been studied, what other researchers find important, various ways this topic has been approached, etc.

Step 3. Field Research and initial interviews:

Here, you connect with your system (organization/community) by visiting the physical location, talking to those involved, and observing routines. Take note of who appears to be the main actors? Who should be involved? Once identified, it is useful to conduct interviews with those key actors that you have identified. Also relevant is the exploration of other organizations/entities or initiatives that might be part of, or related to, this exploration.

What does this context look like?

How do things seem to work here?

Who are the main actors here?

Make a list of relevant people to interview.

Interviewing will begin in this first Phase. However, interviewing can be employed in all design phases. To ensure a useful interview, it is critically important to be familiar with your topic, with your objectives, and with what you want to achieve. From there you can design a collection of questions that orient the interview. Since interviewing is core in any research project, we offer here some options/possible techniques.

Interviewing is a classic method of research. As a researcher, interviews can assist in gaining information about places and people, and gaining access to the reasons people hold specific meanings of life/work events. In traditional research, collecting data requires a controlled environment and a neutral researcher in order to guarantee the validity and the rigor of the data collected.

However, new approaches to research (like the one we are presenting here) challenge this tradition by recognizing that when we enter the research field, we are already influencing the environment and the people by our presence. Furthermore, the type of questions we ask invite particular forms of conversation. Thus, the interview, as a research approach, is focused on collaborative conversation; a conversation with a purpose.

Different types of questions and interviews

The questions you ask and the type of interview you chose to conduct will depend on the topic you are exploring. See below:

Open-ended interviewing.

If your objective is to amplify meanings on a certain topic, an open-ended interview is recommended. This type of interview aids in understanding people's meanings regarding a specific object. For this reason, simple yes/no or fixed-response questions are not useful. Open-ended interviews allow participants to express their thoughts and their understanding using their own words. Open-ended interviews are also particularly valuable in the beginning of your research project, helping to expand the understanding of your topic.

Circular questioning.

More than a type of interview, circular questions offer a way of asking questions. Circular questioning (Selvini, Boscolo, Cecchin & Prata, 1980; Tomm, 1985) generates relational information. These forms of questions are based on Gregory Bateson's (1980) idea that information is a difference and a difference is a relationship. Thus, if we ask, "How long have you been depressed?" the answer is likely to be viewed as "factual" (e.g., "Three months."). Yet, if instead we ask, "If I asked your wife how long you have been depressed, what do you think she would say?" the answer provides information about the relationship (e.g., "She would say since I lost my job."). The wife might disagree and say, "He's been depressed since our only child left home for college." The conversation is directed to the relationship among ideas, people, contexts, etc. and away from a fact-finding expedition. We are no longer "digging" for the "truth" but expanding the perspective on the topic, inviting multiple descriptions.

Mobile interviewing.

A mobile interview is an innovative way to generate data. It is an interview in which you move along the environment with the interviewee. It is a powerful method to explore the space in loco and gain a sense of how those you are interviewing experience the context. Mobile interviewing can yield very different descriptions from those garnered when people talk "about" a context.

You can use this approach when the topic of the research involves a specific space. With mobile interviewing, you use the environment in order to understand your topic. It is important to trust the process of moving around with your interviewee and generate questions as you notice what is happening in the moment.

If you use mobile interviewing, make sure to:

- **Be alongside each other:** converse while facing outward and away from each other – the focus goes beyond each other and is not focused only on the interviewee;
- **Move around:** take advantage of the disruptive space (what are the elements that emerge?);
- **Participants lead:** the participant is in charge and might take you to unexpected places.

It is also important to keep field notes (digital or written) of all the information you are gathering. These field notes are useful as you advance through the various research Phases, as they remind you of the details of the environment and your experience.

Quick tips on interviewing

Try to engage with your participant without suggesting meanings in advance, without forcing your views on the participant. During the conversation, you can explore your topic by asking the question such as:

- What do you mean by ---- (repeat the word or sentence that was just uttered)
- Could you unfold this idea?
- Could you talk more about that?
- Interesting... how did you come to this (idea/image/plan, etc.)?

After going through the three steps described above, you are ready to embrace all the knowledge you have gathered and start designing the collaborative co-creation sessions.

Now, with more clarity on your topic, an understanding of what the literature has to say about it, a bit of understanding through your field research and appreciative interviews, you are ready for some collaborative co-creation. For that you will need to approach specific people based on the information you have just gathered. Your approach should also be appreciative. What does this mean in practice? The search here is for what is valuable in a system. The goal is to discover what elements are working well and functioning effectively in order to help the system grow. At this point, it is important to avoid too much focus on problematic issues. You might be thinking: "if this is research, you shouldn't have such an influence." However, as we already discussed, within the constructionist paradigm, it is impossible to be neutral and objective. The questions we ask, the articles and books we read, the people with whom we talk already define the directions of our research. Given these circumstances, we want to intentionally set an appreciative and productive direction.

Let's look at a simple illustration of how to do that

The description below illustrates two different approaches to food management (inspired by Camargo-Borges, 2019).

A traditional project on food management would likely start with an analysis of the heart of the problem (i.e., food waste) in order to prepare for the next Phase – finding solutions. Thus, you would first collect information about what is wrong. You would investigate the usual sources such as food service and management, food production and product development, supermarkets and other distribution channels, restaurants, hotels and all kinds of industry representatives. You would talk to the people in these areas asking them: "What is wrong? How do you deal with the problem of food waste here?" You would then search the written legislation (literature review) of food as it relates to production, regulation, inspection, and distribution. With this information in hand, you would ask:

• How can we fix management?

• How can we end food waste?

• Why is this causing such disputes concerning small farming and concerning consumption in the food supply chain?

This type of analysis already sets the stage for a focus on food waste as the reason for inequalities and the problem of world hunger. The logical (and typical) next step after this analysis would be to raise awareness of food waste and to invest in education to bring about change. This traditional approach, focusing on what is wrong, has implications. Because the research is centered on "What is the problem," it creates an approach centered on fixing something. Yet, the solution does not necessarily go beyond the problem; it might simply be a temporary fix. It might also create resistance among those involved with the problem since the "solution" might invite them to see themselves as incompetent and in need of education.

On the other hand, by embracing an appreciative analysis, the investigation might start by trying to understand what is working well in this realm. What are some of the most useful achievements in food management? This does not mean ignoring the problems. Rather, your focus will center on elements that help you expand possibilities and design opportunities instead of fixing what is wrong. This approach brings energy rather than resistance, uniting people to support the quest, rather than creating separation and opposition. Questions such as:

- What are the experiences of successful food management?
- What can we learn from best cases in food management ?
- Are there examples of successful small farming in the food supply chain?

Preparing for collaborative co-creation: How Can We Design It?

As we already discussed in Chapter 2 when introducing the Framework, co-creation can function as a concept and as a practice. As a concept – we are co-creators and meaning is fluid and constantly changing – co-creation is a paradigm we embrace throughout the entire research process. As a practice, we engage in co-creation in action, which means "making something together," inviting research participants to experiment with collaborative ways to tackle what is relevant and useful for the research topic.

Designing your Co-Creation Sessions

Participants

Make a list of the core participants who should be invited to the co-creation session. Invite them individually and highlight the importance of their presence. Collective invitations often yield little to no participation since potential participants do not feel their presence is or would be special and unique.

Sample

In order to have a productive conversation, it is generally a good idea to limit the group to approximately eight to ten people. More than this number makes interaction, listening, and co-creating ideas difficult.

Location

Choose the location with care. It is best to have a comfortable place to talk and interact. The location plays an important role in making participants feel safe to give voice to their opinions and ideas. Furthermore, the design of the space is also crucial in stimulating interactions. Make sure participants can see each other (organizing chairs in a circle is a good choice here).

Preparing questions

Reflect upon what truly is the strength of the topic and from there prepare some questions for the conversation. Prepare a few questions (three or four) and invite the participants to engage in an unfolding conversation. Again, if the environment is comfortable (both physically and interpersonally), participants will feel free to add their own beliefs and understandings to the conversation.

Co-creation in action

When starting your session, make sure to give space for participants to become acquainted. An introduction should be offered to the research participants, as well as an opportunity to share expectations (purpose, time commitment, interactions etc.). A personal introduction from each researcher and research participant allows the creation of a safe environment and a sense of belonging to the group, ensuring higher participation. After the introductions of the goals, expectations, and people, the first question can be shared, encouraging discussion and ensuring interaction. You can give research participants time to share their ideas or you could also pair them up, giving them some time to share with their partner and then summarizing later to the group. It is often easier for people who might be less eager to speak up in a group to share their ideas with one another initially.

Leave enough time for each question and also make sure new ones emerge and are discussed. Make notes of potential new questions and experiences and ask the group to explore them.

The co-creative sessions will offer support in combining current ideas with new ones participants bring; by interacting with the research participants, you will also have the opportunity to check if the information you have already gathered makes sense to those involved and from there you will be able to decide what is really important for the project.

Harvesting

After all the questions are discussed, close the session with a harvest. Harvesting is the process of making visible the highlights and outputs of the conversation. There are many tools you can use to harvest, such as graphic harvesting which is synthesizing information into an easy visual image. As you start the harvest process make sure you have a space where everyone can write down their highlights, conclusions, and next steps. In this way, you can guarantee that all voices will be heard and you can make sure everyone is aligned in the conversation and the understanding that has been reached/gained.

Mapping your System - some tools to apply

With all the information gathered in this Phase, you are ready to map the system. Creating a map is a good way to comprehend and visualize the interconnections of the theme, providing a big picture for the next Phases. In mapping, you should include all perspectives and understandings of the topic as well as any information concerning the larger context in which the topic exists. Mapping can also support preparing the research team for the research process.

There are many ways to map your system to create a more complex understanding of your topic. Below we offer some possibilities:

• The rhizomatic mapping: Systems thinking and the rhizomatic approach

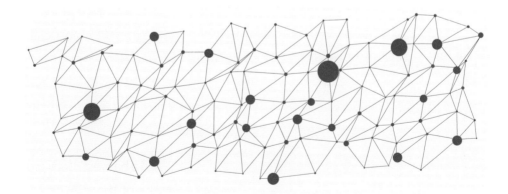

The rhizomatic map is a way to structure and organize your data in an interconnected format, looking at places and people as more than a random collection of parts. It is inspired by the systems thinking approach, which consists of three important components: elements (which could be stakeholders, organizations, and communities), interconnections (the way these elements relate to and/or feed back onto each other), and a function or purpose. Systems thinking involves observing a project – an event or data, in general – and identifying patterns. We are so accustomed to seeing, for example, an organization as a set of isolated parts. We see an organization of management, sales, accounting, marketing, etc. But none of these aspects of an organization make sense without the other aspects. Thus, it is important to understand how they relate to each other and what patterns of interaction are common. By understanding these interconnections, we can create a more useful, contextual, long-term solution to a challenge. Taking a systems approach broadens our thinking and helps us articulate challenges in new and different ways. It is also inspired by the rhizomatic approach. Rhizome is a botanical term. It refers to the root of a plant that pops out of the ground in an expanded way, thereby giving the impression that you are seeing many separate plants emerging in close proximity to one another. However, if you look below the ground, you see that these "apparently" separate plants are actually one common plant. What appear to be separate plants are actually all part of the same root.

Deleuze and Guattari (2013) offer a philosophical understanding of rhizomes. They developed a theory of knowledge, the rhizomatic approach, that metaphorically illustrates the connectivity, heterogeneity, and multiplicity of phenomena that appear isolated, homogeneous, and singular. A rhizome is a centerless network, where every node connects with each other in a horizontal fashion, allowing multiple entry and exit points in a non-hierarchical way. A rhizome has no beginning and no end; it is always in the middle, between elements and always connected, although such connections are not always visible.

When mapping the system in an rhizomatic manner you treat all your information as interconnected and non-hierarchical. It helps you organize and connect the information and ideas, showing the interconnections more explicitly.

· The Empathy Map: focusing on your target group

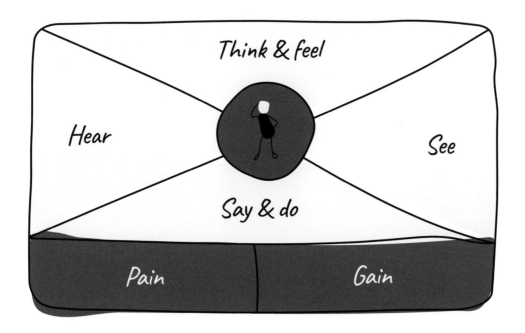

The Empathy Map is more specific to support researchers in better understanding their target group (Gray, Brown, & Macanufo, 2010). With this tool you can understand how the target group perceives the topic being investigated and how they relate to the organization/community. By using this map, you can put yourself in the shoes of your target audience.

The map consists of an image in the center and six quadrants to be completed. You can place the symbol of your target group in the middle of the square. Asking some questions provides answers for each quadrant. Examples of questions you can ask in each quadrant are:

Think and Feel:

This section is about understanding what matters most to the target audience.

- How does your target audience think about this topic?

- What do they wonder about this topic?

- Is your target audience more likely to be connected or disconnected with the topic?

- What do they think about the organization/community you are investigating?

- Do they feel connected to it at all?

Hear and See:

This section is about the influences that impact your target group.

- What are the preferences of your target group?

- In general, how do they see and talk about the topic?

- Are they more into innovative ideas or conservative ones?

- How do they see the organization/community in general?

Say and Do:

This section is about understanding attitudes your target group have towards others.

- What and how do they communicate with others about what they do and like?

- Do they talk about this organization at all?

- What do they say about it?

- What are the actions they take on a day-to-day basis?

- What are their cultural habits?

Pain and Gain:

This section focuses on obstacles that your target group face as well as how they hope to get what they want.

- What frustrates them about their current situation?

- What annoys them?

- Where would they like to be?

- What would they like to do?

- What encourages them?

- What are the good and bad things about the organization in question?

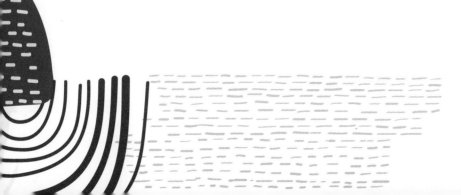

• The Game Plan: An Appreciative Approach to Envisioning a Research Process

If you are working with a team, Game Plan is a design tool that can help you with this first entrance into the research field. It supports the constructions of your research path together with your research team, co-creating a common ground around the project as well as assisting you on where to focus, what the core goals are, and how to start exploring the topic. Through a dynamic process of envisioning the possible directions and looking at the skills of each member of the team, the team can co-create a visual appreciative plan – an image of the research project – including preliminary planning and organizing the next steps. Clear communication and a common plan are central points for a research project and the Game Plan facilitates both and encourages the team to make explicit all the ideas, possibilities and intentions for the project, which then helps with alignment. To map the research path, the team should sit together and go through the Game Plan process, discussing each part of it, creating a visual.

The outcome of the Game Plan is a shared image, a map that helps generate a collective understanding of the research and the Framework of challenges and contexts within which the team can take action. It invites the team to commit and stay aligned throughout the process. The Game Plan does not need to be followed rigidly; it can be a guiding document that helps when change is needed.

The visual here is an adaptation of the Game Plan designed by the KaosPilot, Denmark and the Performatory from Breda university of Applied Sciences. https://www.performatory.nl/

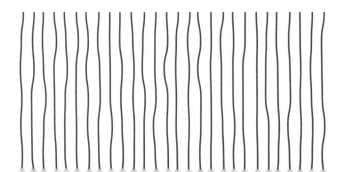

The Game Plan
an appreciative approach

Last but not least
- Think of your role as researcher

In this Framework, the researcher has an important role in enabling co-creation. Here are some of the competences that are required from the researcher to facilitate the collaborative co-creation:

challenge the taken-for-granted: as a researcher, look at all ideas and information offered by the participants as new, fresh, and with an openness and curiosity.

inspire participants to explore and experiment with new ways of talking: add follow up questions inviting participants to talk more about their topic and from different perspectives. You can ask provocative questions, circular questions, etc.

embrace ambiguity and contradiction (to expand meaning).

evoke an open-minded state leading consequently to meaning-making: be curious about what is discussed.

think of yourself as a change agent rather than a "researcher discovering a solution to a problem."

We end this Constructionist-Design Phase 1 with a follow up of the research path

Constructionist-Design Research Phase 1:
Collaborative Co-creation

Play around with your initial ideas	Describe your topic. What do you want to know? Why do you want to know that? What is the relevance of this topic for you and for the system? Who is involved?
Start your literature review	What is the purpose, focus and the central terms related to your topic? Add Keywords for your topic.
Field Research, Initial interviews, Co-creative sessions	Observe the system: where do I need to go? What type of interview would be useful? Craft appreciative questions.
Collaborative co-creative sessions	Participants/Sample: Deciding on who should be present. How many? Location: Choose the location with care. Find a good environment for talking. Prepare questions: Powerful and inspiring question to ignite conversations. Harvest: Connect and highlight your outputs.
Curate your findings by Mapping your System	Systemic-rhizomatic map; The empathy map; The game plan.

Final questions for reflection and application to your project:

- When you think of your research project, what are the first keywords that come into your mind?
- Which of the design tools can support you to stimulate co-creation and promote new meanings?
- Which of the design tools described in this chapter do you see yourself using? Why?

Define and Reframe
Creating Generative Research Questions in Research Phase 2

This chapter will introduce:

- Framing and reframing - how to connect ideas and create a productive "container"
- How to make new interpretations and reinterpretations
- What framing research questions are crucial to an investigation
- What is generative theory
- What are generative research questions
- What is a challenge statement in research and how to design one

The research process continues with defining and reframing your topic. In the second Constructionist-Design Research Phase you will engage in framing and reframing the co-created results of the first Phase. Now that you know more about your topic from different perspectives and angles – now that you know "what is the case" based on your investigation and conversations – it is time to bring this knowledge to the creation of generative research questions.

While the first Phase was designed to assist you in gaining a deeper understanding and appreciation of the topic, the second Phase will help you frame this understanding and appreciation into powerful research questions that will guide the inquiry process.

In this Phase, you will explore different combinations of your already gathered information, framing and reframing the ideas. By exploring various frames for your topic, you can develop a more complex, nuanced, and detailed understanding which will assist you in making your initial research questions stronger and thus more powerful, what we refer to as generative research questions.

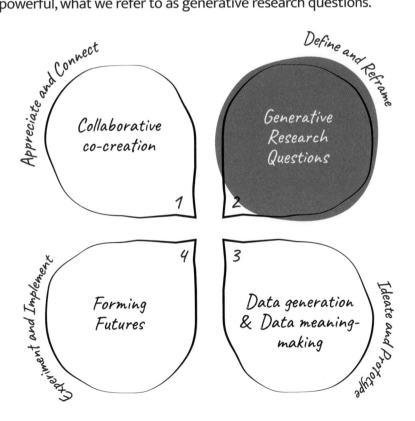

For a number of years, framing has been used in social sciences (Goffman, 1974; Entman, 1993; Benford & Snow, 2000) and can be defined as the process of finding a coherent combination of all the identified ideas and knowledge, uniting them together. You frame and reframe by selecting relevant aspects of the information and connecting them into a whole. It is also a strategic process of providing shared problem definition, recognizing and connecting perspectives, as well as observing nuances.

Framing is about connecting ideas and creating a productive "container" but also it is about offering new interpretations that might lead to reinterpretations and thus reframing. This process of tacking back and forth will eventually offer direction to a research process, consequently supporting decision making in the stages that follow.

A design attitude toward framing and reframing always starts with challenging the status quo, which means challenging how a problem has already been framed. The design attitude plays with the process of framing and reframing to give space for other ways to understand, while also providing opportunities for the emergence of new ways of talking about the topic. Within the design thinking approach, defining and reframing are the beginning of the ideation Phase where all the information from the first Phase is reframed into a central (high) concept that guides the research toward the creation of spaces and the design of products, services, and experiences. In design thinking, a high concept has the power to concentrate all important elements into one word or sentence (or sometimes a visual) that creates the image of the concept/project. What design thinking refers to as a "high concept," we identify as our generative research questions, since in research this is what guides the path towards data collection, analysis, and all the findings and decision making. It is the concentration of all the elements that need to be investigated. Our research questions are our guiding star for the research process.

Let's explore how we can start defining and reframing the initial research ideas into a high concept (i.e., a generative research question).

As an example, let's consider again the food management story discussed in Chapter 3. We shared the two different approaches on the topic of food: one more traditional, related to problems and focusing on how to fix those problems and a second alternative, the appreciative approach, where focus is placed on what gives life to the system, meaning what works well, and – as a consequence – centering our attention on possibilities. We looked at what works well in food management. In the first Phase, we explored the topic from this appreciative approach, expanding our understanding. From there, in this second research Phase, we frame and reframe the food management ideas in an attempt to generate research questions. From this process we reframe what is commonly referred to as food waste into food sharing. That could be our initial high concept. The underlying principle here could be that food belongs to all of us, thus we can move from the idea of waste to the notion of sharing. This small alteration changes the perspective from "who is to blame?" to "we are all involved." With this new framing, the issue becomes part of a global system in which we are all responsible for taking action. This appreciative reframing brings inspiration for something new with possibilities rather than fixing what is wrong. It also takes the research topic in the direction of exploring advocacy and social contributions. We can start looking for information that proposes the idea of food as sharing. A good example is the slow food movement (www.slowfood.com) which is centered on valuing local food resources, taking the time to appreciate them, and preserving the ecosystem. Another illustration is the "from farm to table" movement (fromfarmtotable.ca) which promotes the direct acquisition of food from the producer. Finally, we have the example of the Oz harvest project, which is a perishable food rescue organization in Australia collecting food that would not otherwise be used and delivering it free of charge to charities (www.ozharvest.org).

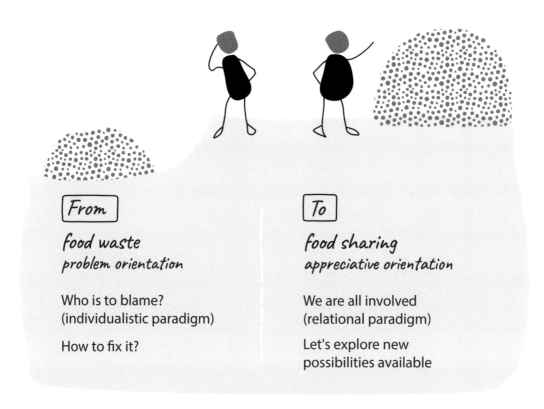

From

food waste
problem orientation

Who is to blame?
(individualistic paradigm)

How to fix it?

To

food sharing
appreciative orientation

We are all involved
(relational paradigm)

Let's explore new
possibilities available

Shifting to the idea of sharing food rather than the lack of food or wasting food is part of this effort to define and reframe in this Phase. This exercise is generative in the ways that it opens the possibility for rich research questions with productive paths to follow. Note that the issue started with problems in food management and, through the process of reframing, we can now view the research topic in a completely different way. Food waste calls for a more individualistic, rational, and hierarchical attitude to solve the problem. It is similar to the ecological recycling movement where individuals are expected to recycle plastic but the corporations that package goods and food in plastic continue to produce environmentally harming materials. Food sharing, as opposed to food waste, involves the whole system and everyone in it. It entails relational and ethical responsibility (McNamee, 2010) where everybody is responsible for what happens to food. It invites engagement in which the social actors involved search for alternatives. This example illustrates how the appreciative component in the first Phase supports and links with the framing and reframing of the second Phase, producing a generative potential for the research endeavor.

Once we shift from a problem orientation to an appreciative orientation, we can frame generative questions.

Reframing assists in developing a focus for the research project. Each framing will lead to a specific focus and thus specific directions.

Curiosity about how an organization initiates the food sharing approach might extend to a curiosity concerning the logistics of an organization's process or management. This will lead to a focus on management and an interest in the managerial logistics of the supply chain. Or, instead, you might want to know how employees become involved and inspired by the organization's process or management which would require a focus on employee perspectives.

It is important to remember that your questions must have focus and should not be overly broad or lacking reference to the specific context.

Why are research questions so crucial in an investigation?

A well-framed question makes your research clear and explicit. It is important to remember that there is never one "correct" research question. There are always multiple questions and the one you choose to work with will direct your research in different ways thereby constructing different results, solutions, and possibilities. Rather than look for the "right" question, ask yourself, "How might this question be useful to the community with which I am working?"

While it might seem excessive to spend one full Phase of the research framing and reframing your topic in order to construct questions, the design of coherent, comprehensible questions is crucial to the success of any research.

Creating generative questions supports the unfolding process of research and assists in defining tasks, actions, and the overall approach towards your investigation. Your research questions serve as a constant guide and reference, keeping the research process on track.

As you progress through your research process, you will find yourself constantly tacking back and forth between your data and your questions, to see if you are adequately addressing the questions and tackling the topic properly. This is especially important because, when you start with your data generation process, there will be a multitude of perspectives, ideas, and points of view that have the potential to distract from your primary goal. If or when this happens, the research questions are there to keep you on track. Strong generative questions are fundamental to ensuring that you don't get lost in this iterative process.

We must add, though, that questions are never fixed, never set "once and for all." Research questions can change during the research process as new information emerges together with new understandings of the issue, which might in turn require another attempt at reframing (Creswell, 2007). This is part of the iterative process of research. It is always good to have a team (your supervisor or a research group) with whom you can discuss the need to reframe your questions, thereby setting off another iterative process of tacking back and forth between your research questions and your gathering of new information.

Let us show you what this iterative process might look like using the illustration of food management again. Imagine your generative research question is: "How can we enable the process of sharing food in the food chain?" When initiating your data generation within this frame, as you explore your question, you are met with participants' frustrations with issues of transporting food from its local source for distribution. At this point, you might want to reflect on the centrality of transportation to the idea of sharing food. The specific issue of transportation now needs to be integrated into your research questions. You can make an alignment by slightly changing your question into: "How does transportation help or hinder the expansion of food sharing?" This alignment is important as it reminds you of the centrality of transportation as you move forward into data collection.

Generative theory and questions – the constructionist approach

Knowledge within a constructionist perspective has a relational dimension as it is seen as a co-achievement where researchers and participants engage in a certain venture that collaboratively produces meaning. Knowledge has its roots in shared interactions with others, gained through exchanges, relationships, and dialogue (Gergen & Gergen, 2004). The collaborative production of knowledge is characterized by processes of deconstruction and reconstruction, resulting in what is called "generative theory" (Gergen 1994; 1978). Generative theory is theory that creates new possibilities and it contrasts with the idea of theory as looking "backward" as a process of discovery. Here, theory is looking forward where new creations emerge; it is then future-forming and, therefore, generative, creating new meanings, actions and possibilities.

Taking that constructionist understanding into account, we then focus on generative questions and approaches to knowledge development that have the potential to broaden our taken-for-granted beliefs and behaviors of the local culture, thereby opening up the potential for further explorations, novel action potentials, and social change.

Questions here have the generative capacity to provoke the search for new understanding, directions, practices, and behaviors. Thus, generative research questions promote more creative and productive possibilities.

We are not saying that initial frames are wrong. The point of framing and reframing is to expand the range of generative questions. We move away from the idea of a single root problem with one possible answer and we open up for a multiplicity of options to explore. With that, our data becomes richer, creating more productive paths.

By selecting participants and framing and asking our questions, we are already co-creating new possibilities. When we understand that, we acknowledge that a research process is a form of social intervention/transformation as we are already setting the stage for reflections, dialogue, and opportunities for new configurations of the system. We are not simply promoting knowledge about the system; we are already moving researchers and participants toward newly constructed futures. As Seelig (2013, n.p.) states :

"All questions are the frame into which the answers fall. By changing the frame, you can dramatically change the range of possible solutions."

With this quote, we realize that generative research questions are not just questions searching for an answer but invite openings and also propose different understandings of a problem.

How can we go about framing and reframing the topic, and transforming our framing into a generative research question(s)?

By blending social construction and design thinking, we offer some ways to play with framing and reframing.

There are many ways to reframe a topic. Each way will have implications for the continuation of your research process and the kind of decisions you will make in the next Phases. If you look at the dots below as representing different information from Phase I, you might form different images (understanding) of the topic, depending upon how you map (connect) your information.

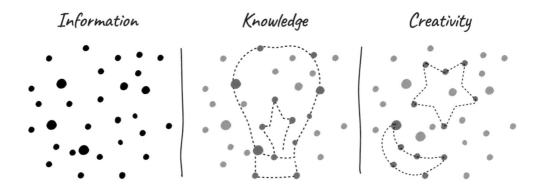

Information   Knowledge   Creativity

With these new understandings, you can frame, reframe, and finally write generative research questions for your study. Have a look here at two examples of tools that can help you frame and reframe to start defining your generative research question.

Framing and Reframing tools

• First tool: Mapping Positions

This first tool is about taking the information you have gathered and reflecting on it from different positions and perspectives. A good starting place for this exercise is to separate the ideas into what was said by your stakeholders, what you found in your desk research, and your reflections on both; What were the actions you saw and how did you feel about them. This exercise can help you identify what has been collaboratively co-created. It can also help you, the researcher, develop some ideas concerning the implications of various directions to follow. In addition, this exercise invites you to pay attention to the commonly held beliefs about the topic and explore alternative explanations and further meaning about which it might be important to know more. With that, you expand understanding, thereby clarifying possible directions to follow.

Here is how you do it. Take a look at your findings from the first Phase and try to fill in the spaces:

Mapping Positions

Affirmations...

What statements can you make from the information you already have?

_____
_____
_____
_____
_____
_____
_____
_____

Reflections...

What other thoughts or different interpretations come to mind? What points call attention to you and need further reflection?

_____
_____
_____
_____
_____
_____
_____

Feelings...

When you think about your topic, what kind of sensations do you have? What do you feel and where do you feel it?

_____
_____
_____
_____
_____
_____
_____
_____

Doubts...

What doubts come to mind?
What is still uncertain about the topic?

_____
_____
_____
_____
_____
_____

This is an exercise in which you could actually engage in any Phase of your research (actually in any situation to clarify your thoughts and positions). It helps with illuminating ideas, expanding them, and supporting you when you get stuck.

• Second tool: Generating Reframes

This tool can help to generate a number of keywords. It is very simple and powerful as keywords are useful ways to organize and structure specific content, assisting in developing a frame on a particular concept. It is a good way to create meaningful content maps by combining central ideas and being able to play around reframing the content, thereby landing on strong concepts. You start by adding a variety of keywords related to the information you have. From there you narrow your focus by connecting the words and from the connection reframing into new ones. Directions will emerge showing concepts and content that fit the combination of the keywords. The strength of this tool is that, with a quick glance, you can see the central, relevant concepts and gain a picture of connections and interconnections.

Generating Reframes

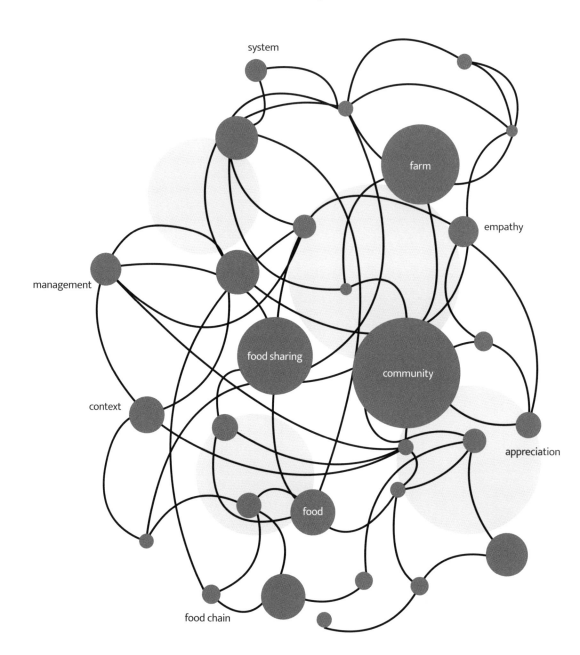

system

farm

empathy

management

food sharing

community

context

appreciation

food

food chain

Framing-Reframing: Generative Research Questions

Once you have played with the tools above, thinking and rethinking, framing and reframing, giving focus and direction, then, you are ready to create generative research questions.

When framing your ideas into a question, pay attention to creating research questions that are truly generative and not just typical questions coming from traditional research. What do we mean by that? Traditional research elaborates a problem statement, results from the literature review, and defines questions seeking a definitive answer to a complicated issue.

Generative questions are more open-ended and encourage a wider view that is not driving at a single solution but rather is in search of an integrative approach that would incorporate already existing knowledge and structures with those emerging in the present research.

We move here from the classic Problem Statement to the Challenge Statement Design. The following chart can help you organize the reframed ideas - outcome of Phase 2 - and set them into generative research questions.

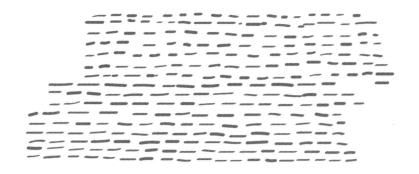

From Problem Statement to Challenge Statement Design

The issue of...	Describe here the challenge you have in the way that was presented to you.
Could be reframed into...	Describe the shift you made when reframing; identify a different understanding of the problem; write a different aspect or perspective of it.
Brings the opportunity/possibility	What can you see anew? Moving from — to— Describe what might emerge that is new. What are the implications of this?
Benefits of this investigation would be...	Describe what you imagine might happen when developing this research. What could be the impact of this investigation?

Generative Research Question(s):
Describe here what your question becomes.

Let's take the example of food management and do an exercise with this chart.

⊐ **The issue of .....**Food waste as a global problem, creating not just starvation among the more vulnerable but also contributing to food insecurity, global warming, and climate change.

⊐ **Could be reframed into....** Sharing food. The idea of sharing food can demonstrate the value of both growing food and building community. It can provide opportunities for people to become small producers, and learn how to cultivate a garden. It could also provide food solutions for a revitalized agricultural economy and a healthier food chain. That would, in turn, provide nutritious food across the world.

⊐ **Brings the opportunity/possibility....** To move from an unsustainable world of starvation, overconsumption, waste, and climate challenges to a world of opportunities where many initiatives create value in the food chain by learning how to garden, reuse waste, recycle into useful products, and optimize processes.

⊐ **Benefits of this investigation would be.....** That new businesses and innovative opportunities in sharing food might initiate regenerative practices from which farmers can learn and consumers can buy, thereby creating more sustainable practices. Potential sustainable practices might include new relationships in the food value chain, collaborative processes to achieve global resources and to deliver locally, redistribution of food to eliminate poverty and hunger, adaptation of crops to current climate change, ability to address issues of climate change, and community building.

All these resources together enable an understanding of the topic, allowing you to envision what you really want to know and how to create your generative research question. By organizing your learning/information into a structured "problem statement," a generative research question could be formed:

⊐ **Generative Research question:** "How do we build on current food projects to enhance the production and distribution networks focusing on sustainable developments in food management?"

Here are some more quick examples to frame and reframe using different topics and transforming them into generative questions. Can you see the differences?

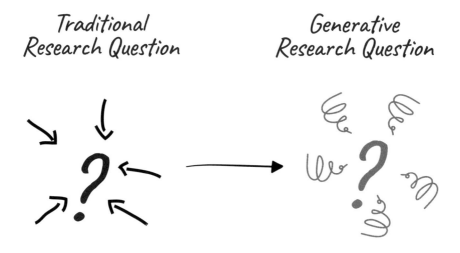

Traditional
Research Question

Generative
Research Question

Traditional research question: "What are the structures needed in a city to develop a sustainable destination?"

Generative question: "How do we build on current city structures and relationships to enhance sustainable developments of a destination?"

The difference between these two questions is that the first one focuses on specific structures that the research imagines are necessary to create sustainability, while the second question is more interested in exploring what is already happening and connecting to sustainable practices. It is about creating knowledge in context.

- - - - - - - - - - - -

Traditional research question: "Can we afford increasing care and treatment for an aging population?"

Generative question: "What are the existing forms of treatment and care for our aging population that are working well? How might we amplify this sort of care?"

Notice that the first question invites a limited response; either we can afford increased care and treatment or we cannot. The second question invites participants to pool their creative and innovative ideas about care.

Traditional research question: "What governance structures do we need to create in order to improve education?"

Generative question: "How can we enhance and utilize the structures, resources, and processes already present to improve equity and effectiveness of education?"

Similarly, the first question assumes that the researcher can identify the "right" structures needed to improve education while the second question opens the researcher and participants to a myriad of ideas.

Traditional research question: "How can we improve student performance in high stakes testing?"

Generative question: "What are we learning from current assessments? What are the areas and practices that enliven both students and teachers? How can we borrow from these successes and bring them to the context of testing?"

Finally, with the first question, we are looking for concrete strategies that will guarantee testing success. The second question asks us to consider what we really are learning about the assessment process and its utility.

Using Your Generative Research Question to Make Methodological Choices

The generative research question is a navigation tool that can help a researcher delineate possible directions while giving support when the unexpected might emerge. The second Phase of the Constructionist-Design Research Framework ends with framing your generative research questions. In this context, a strong generative research question(s) becomes the "high concept" of the project, opening a vision for the research project and process in the sense that you can now move forward with the best methodological choices based on the purpose of the research.

Now you are ready to write a brief summary of possible directions to be taken. Look at the chart and start preparing your methodology. See the critical decisions to be made, what to consider and write down your decisions.

Making the Transition:
from Generative Questions to Methodological Choices

Critical decisions to be made...	To consider	Your decisions
Generative Research Question	The research question(s) become your guide for the following discussions.	
Participants	Those who will be participating in your research will be determined by your framing of the research question(s).	
Place	In what space/place are your participants most likely to feel comfortable (familiar) and able to participate?	
Data Generation Methods	What kind of data would be useful to gather? How do you imagine gathering your data?	
Data Meaning-Making	How do you imagine interpreting your data?	

Final questions for reflection and application to your project:

- We invite you to practice reframing your research topic by using some of the tools we offer in this Chapter.

- Look at your research questions and try to transform them into generative questions by using the Challenge Statement Design.

- Transition from your generative questions to your methodological choices, using the chart provided as a guide.

V

Ideate and Prototype
Data Generation & Data Meaning Making in Research Phase 3

This chapter will introduce:

- How to generate data from your research project
- How to make meaning from your gathered data
- A variety of creative tools/method for data generation and data meaning-making
- Researcher as a change agent; a co-creative catalyst of the research process
- How to design research with quality

Introduction

Having created generative research questions in Design Phase 2, we move forward to Phase 3 of the research Framework, data generation and data meaning-making. It is also the Phase in which we ideate and prototype. In the language of research, this is your methodology.

In this Chapter we will explore what ideate and prototype mean for your research project. We will present a constructionist methodology, showing how the research method unfolds, how the researcher is also a change agent, and how you can provide a rationale for the quality of your project (which is crucial when writing a report). Methods borrowed from design thinking will be offered as creative tools to support you in this meaning-making Phase.

Through data generation and data meaning-making, a variety of ideas and possibilities will emerge. This Phase ends with the selection of ideas for a prototype where you can begin to test the prototype's feasibility, crafting a plan for experimentation and implementation (Phase 4).

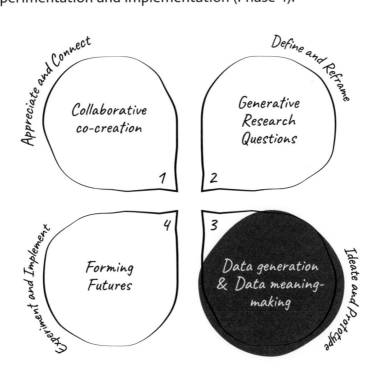

Methodology

Let's start with methodology. In classic research, methodology is the process of discovering and further understanding what your context is and what participants do/think of the research topic. In constructionist research, we go beyond this. Methodology is focused on envisioning and unfolding new possibilities not yet imagined. To the constructionist, the methodology section of research is about expanding the views on a given topic, generating and exploring new information, ideas, and stories. In order to accomplish this, the researcher cannot be at the service of established questions and rigid methods. The methodological process, for a Constructionist-Design researcher, is not about discovering but about creating. Thus, the methods do not dominate the research process. They are instead understood as facilitating the knowledge process that is yet to be developed within the very specific context of any given research project. A methodology, inspired by the Constructionist-Design approach, is conducted without imposing pre-determined techniques or assumptions, which means that the methods do not drive the inquiry. Rather the context of the inquiry (and the participants involved) will define the methods. Within this logic, there is no ultimate best method for a given research project; rather, each method will produce specific (and different) information. Asking different questions will construct different knowledge. This attitude toward research requires a dynamic process of participatory investigation and interpretation, where researchers and participants remain open, flexible, and empathic. As Gersick proposes, "Get all the help you can from existing methods, but be willing to try making up something new" (Gersick, 2016, p. 317). This is a move from 'methods of research' to 'practices of inquiry" (Gergen, 2014).

Traditional research

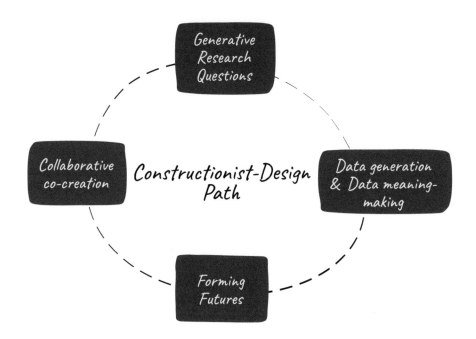

Generative Research Questions

Collaborative co-creation

Constructionist-Design Path

Data generation & Data meaning-making

Forming Futures

Methods: data generation and data meaning-making

In the realm of practices of inquiry we are not focused on the right method, presuming that it will lead to the discovery of the reality. As a collaborative process, we search for a method that will facilitate interaction and conversation on the topic we are investigating. While there is no ultimate, right method, there are methods that – for a variety of reasons – serve as a better fit for the topic being researched and the context of the research. The same goes for data meaning-making. The ways in which we make sense of data are not discovery of something that is already there waiting for the research to reveal. The interpretation of data (meaning-making) is an emergent process, bound and guided by the research questions.

Design thinking, with its creative and participatory methods, make a great combination with the social constructionist understanding of methodology and can offer powerful tools for innovative data generation and data meaning-making.

Data collection versus data generation

Because we do not presume that our research will uncover some truth or fact that already exists, we do not adopt the notion that we are collecting data. Rather, as we mentioned earlier, the questions we ask and the methods we employ generate data. Should we select different questions and/or different methods, we would generate different data. This distinction reminds us to be attentive to what sorts of data our questions and methods might be inviting. It also reminds us to be curious about what alternative questions and methods might yield. But our curiosity is not directed toward answering the question: which is right? Rather, our curiosity is directed toward the question: which might be most generative to this community, in this context, at this time?

Data analysis versus data meaning-making

With these understandings, we reframe data collection into data generation and data analysis into data meaning-making. This shift has an enormous consequence on how we look at data. Using traditional methodologies, we collect data and analyze it. Data, in this case, is the fact waiting to be revealed by the sharp methods of the researcher. That means, if we use the right method, we will discover the investigated reality.

Data collection

Data generation

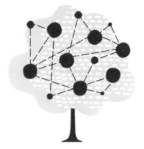

Data analysis

Data meaning-making

For us, within the Constructionist-Design Research Framework, the research method is understood as a performance, as a way to make sense (McNamee, 2010). The researcher is encouraged to ask, reflectively and creatively, questions that might not yet have been asked.

The researcher is encouraged to ask how a given topic or situation could or might change. There is no assumption that there are facts waiting to be revealed. Rather, research is viewed as a process of reflection and co-creation, investigating unspoken assumptions while remaining responsive to the research participants.

That is why we prefer to talk about data generation as opposed to data collection. Data is always generated in relationship with the researcher, the participants, the methods, and the context. It is never simply collected. We co-produce data and we make sense of data in accordance with the theories and values we are holding. Each time we enter a system (organization or community) we are already affecting the system. Each time we formulate one question to ask research participants we are actively provoking reflection and ideas. Thus, data generation is also a meaning-making process and is crucial to generate useful information for any research project.

Of course, our interpretation of data is our attempt to answer our research questions. Traditional data analysis presumes that the research is transforming the "raw" data collected into discovered facts. However, in the Constructionist-Design Research Framework, the researcher is acknowledged as making meaning of the data. We are not searching for the ultimate universal truth, a stable fact waiting to be discovered. In social constructionist terms, meaning is a good replacement for facts and figures. If our understanding of the world and what we take to be real are constructions made in communities by people in their encounters, then there is no such thing as fact in the sense of a universal or isolated "thing." Facts are always created at some point in time, and are located historically and culturally, always in relation to the political and social context. If we are replacing our focus on facts with a focus on meaning, then our data analysis can be redefined as data meaning-making since we will always make interpretations within contexts.

While we draw this distinction between data generation and data meaning-making, it is important to be aware that these processes might transpire in synchronicity. The interpretation Phase of data already begins as we generate the data, since we are already creating ideas and meanings.

Creative sessions in design thinking:
Dialogue and Co-creation

Creative sessions are a typical and recurrent affair in design, comprising part of this Framework as well (as you have seen in Phase 1 already - collaborative co-creation). It is usually a coming together of people involved to creatively understand an issue better and to create a base for collaboration. In doing so, sharing common ground becomes possible.

In design thinking, creative sessions take the form of participatory working formats designed to provoke new ideas and meanings of a project. They are often used to elicit "out of the box" ideas. We add a constructionist flavor to the design idea of a creative session by emphasizing dialogue and co-creation.

Dialogue here is not defined in general terms as ordinary conversation. Dialogue focuses on a very special way of relating. Dialogue is an ongoing interactive process where the focus is on the potential of sharing multiple local realities (Gergen, McNamee & Barrett, 2001). Placing dialogue within the design process of creative sessions, for example, invites all perspectives that research participants bring; all the different understandings on a topic are invited and shared. Finding the "best opinion" or achieving "the best solution" is not a matter of an accurate and rational description of the "real world," but is the byproduct of a dynamic dialogic process that takes into account the cultural, historical, and situated aspects of each participant's point of view. Therefore, through dialogue, the possibilities of considering different backgrounds and understandings that might invite alternatives are accepted and encouraged. Researcher and research participants together, in dialogue, entertain ideas and understandings that can be combined, created, and re-created.

Dialogue promotes a space for true co-creation, where participants bring a multiplicity of voices, thereby creating a process that is intimately connected with entertaining new realities (Gergen, McNamee & Barrett, 2001). Bakhtin (1981) emphasizes the way in which dialogue embraces multiple voices and welcomes diversity of relations, thereby promoting creative processes. Our values and belief systems expand and change as we are immersed and open for these sharing moments. This is because, instead of our often taken for granted persuasive way of engaging with others where we want to impose our beliefs and values on them, dialogue is not focused on persuasion.

Dialogue is infused with curiosity and respect for different views, values, and beliefs. Therefore, participants are more likely to expand and transform their own views, values, and beliefs.

Dialogue is viewed as a core process in Design Phase 3. Here, the co-creative environment offers the potential for new ideas. In the process of co-creating within the creative sessions, participants, with the facilitation of the researcher, develop stories about the topic offered. Co-creation favors pluralism, allowing multiple voices to emerge thereby encouraging diversity (Camargo-Borges & Rasera, 2013). Through this process, new meanings often promote new ideas.

Dialogue versus Debate

We also emphasize here that dialogue is very different from debate. In a debate, there is an exchange of views and positions where the attempt is to discern which of the competing views is most rational. The aim in debate is to persuade or convince others. With our focus on dialogue and co-creation, the process of relating and interacting with the research participants takes precedence; by creating opportunities for dialogue, meaningful conversations can generate new possible realities.

In this Chapter we share some creative tools for data generation and data meaning-making; tools to trigger and enact conversation, creativity, and new ideas. However, as a researcher, you must be attentive to how you facilitate the process such that creativity and innovation emerge. In this approach to research, the researcher is implicated in the process and does not adopt a neutral or objective stance (as claimed in conventional research).

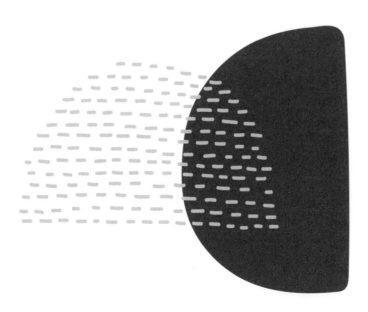

Researcher as a change agent

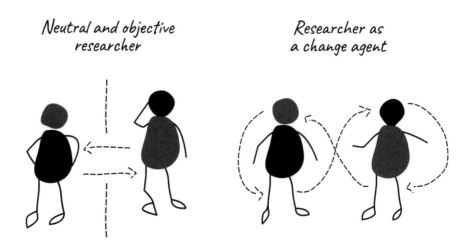

Neutral and objective researcher

Researcher as a change agent

The classic subject-object separation in research does not apply within the Constructionist-Design Research Framework. Here, researchers and participants are not in opposition. Conventional research emphasizes a neutral and objective researcher. In our Framework, the researcher is engaged and adopts the position of change agent (Czarniawska, 2004). The researcher intentionally provokes interactions and reflections concerning the research process itself. We have already mentioned the important role the researcher has in Chapter 3, when discussing interviews. Here, again, as we talk about creative sessions, dialogue, and co-creation in research, we have to emphasize the importance of the researcher.

An engaged researcher generates potential in the research process by attending to what is unfolding moment by moment. Rather than follow a predetermined path (method, technique), the engaged researcher – because of his/her attentiveness to the ongoing process of interaction – generates emergent and organic dynamics (Schnitman, 2010). This is distinctive from a researcher who follows previously determined questions (e.g., validated questionnaires). By attending to the unfolding process, the engaged researcher is able to tap into what is created in the moment.

The researcher can also be seen as a facilitator of co-creative processes, a co-creative catalyst (Tuyl, 2009) for emerging new meanings and ideas. This means that, rather than behaving as neutral and objective, the researcher takes advantage of his/her role and facilitates the co-creation of new perceptions, new points, and scenarios, thereby serving as catalyst for potential transformation.

The engaged researcher or a co-creative catalyst also facilitates the engagement and involvement of the research participants. This is a crucial role of the researcher since the research participants are those who will continue with the transformation when the researcher ends the project and leaves the community/organization. Thus, it is important that research participants believe that the topic and what is co-created is important and would be beneficial to implement.

The engaged researcher and the creative sessions

With an understanding of creative sessions, dialogue, co-creation, and the notion of the researcher as a change agent, we move to action. Creative sessions can be generated with different resources, which we share here. However, more important than the resources used is how the researcher facilitates the interaction and the process of generating data and meaning-making. This is why the position of the engaged researcher is so important. Curiosity, empathy, powerful questions, and reflexivity are vital in this research Phase.

It is important here to create a safe relational environment. The creative session can take the form of a group activity, but it also could entail individual interviews.

In Chapter 3 we discussed interviews in the appreciating Phase. However, interviews can also be useful in different phases of the research. Interviews here involve the dynamic interplay of talking and listening. Interviews should create a relational space where understanding can be expanded and new ideas on the topic can emerge. The safe environment increases the chance for interviewees to speak openly and freely about their own experiences and lives, enriching the research process and generating mutual understanding on data and how to move forward.

The new meanings that emerge in this Phase of data generation and data meaning-making will be framed into possible solutions, changes, or whatever the goal of the research-project is. In design thinking, we call this a prototype. A prototype in design thinking is the creation of a draft version – based on the findings – of a possible action, product, or service. A prototype allows a quick 'trying out' of the findings, ideas, and meanings created. With that we can also invite feedback on the creation (prototype).

Ideate and prototype with creative sessions

In our research context, we embrace the design approach of the creative sessions to engage all research participants in dialogue and co-creation. Using the materials found in the first phases of the design process, participants are invited to imagine multiple futures, to connect with their personal stories, as well as with the context of the research.

The design tools, combined with the philosophical ideas of meaning-making, co-creation, and dialogue, present new opportunities for innovation in research, exploring different possibilities, transforming existent situations, and creating preferred ones (Villar-Guhl, 2014).

Below we share some design thinking tools for data generation, data meaning-making, and how to finalize both into the creation of a prototype.

Creative and innovative methods for data generation

Design thinking offers creative and innovative resources that match well with the social constructionist view on methodology and methods.

When you look at data as meaning and interactions as meaning-making processes, then your methods need creative and inventive formats.

We might describe this as a shift away from traditional methods that are pre-planned and designed by the researcher to participatory, co-created methods. Organizing dialogues where participants can create a space to engage in imaginative and metaphorical conversations enhances the generation of new meaning. The creative sessions outlined by design thinking – with the aim of bringing people together – can be easily adapted to data generation and data meaning-making. These methods unleash creativity by encouraging participants to think and interact in novel ways, through innovative working formats.

Here we illustrate some resources (methods) that can be used during this Phase:

Storyboard, Photovoice, and the Six Thinking Hats.

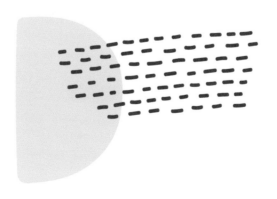

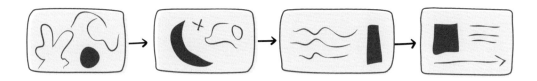

Is a narrative approach to data generation inviting multiple voices in the format of storytelling. These multiple voices bring complexity to the topic. Instead of generating one final solution or result, the idea is to embrace complexity in order to make new understandings, thereby inviting new meanings to emerge.

Here, a creative session with about 8 to 10 participants is organized. The group develops a collective visual story to explore the topic in a narrative format. Research participants raise ideas and connect them to form new meanings. You simply need a wall to co-create the board and a piece of paper or sticky notes. Each research participant takes a few minutes to write one idea. This idea does not need to be a complete thought. It can be one sentence, one quote, or even one word. What is important here is to start collecting the ideas and arranging them on the storyboard. The participants share their ideas and decide how to organize them into one coherent narrative. New meanings start to emerge while participants also share the whys and how's of their own ideas. An overarching view begins to form and new stories begin to arise.

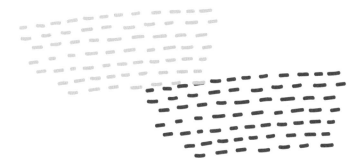

Photography and Photovoice

Social Construction and Design Thinking also gain inspiration from art forms. Use of the creative arts, such as dance, painting, and photography offer alternative ways of addressing research questions. The integration of the arts and research can promote a participatory research path where new ideas and articulations might emerge (Leavy, 2020). For example, we might explore how visual art serves as a method of exposing and altering unequal relations of power, privilege, and oppression. How might researchers use the visual arts for studying race, class, gender, and sexuality?

There are several good examples, but to identify one, we can note how photography can explore cultural perceptions in Africa through the eyes of children (Camargo-Borges, 2017). Using photovoice, which is a method utilizing photographs taken and selected by participants, we had children from Entebbe and Mukono moving around the city taking pictures of what they saw/interpreted as the beauty of Uganda. Using this method, respondents can reflect upon and explore the reasons and experiences that have guided their chosen images.

How does photovoice work in practice? Participants attend a briefing session where the project is presented and together with the researchers align their needs and expectations. The children (in the present example) are then provided with cameras and instructions for using the cameras. Participants were able to explore locations, documenting and revealing what they appreciated about

Uganda and what they wanted to share. The project, named 'Discovering the Beauty of Uganda,' had the goal of engaging in an exploration of the community through the youth's positive experiences and impressions of Uganda. Using the photographs of the research participants, a creative session was organized to co-created meaning together (data meaning-making). In these sessions, participants express their perspective on, views about, and feelings around the topic. The interaction promoted the emergence of new ideas and material with which the researchers and participants worked afterwards. The method enabled participants to generate data on the topic but also invited interaction among themselves as well as with the researchers and their own city, promoting a sense of ownership with their locality.

The pictures were then printed based on choices of participants and together they created stories based on the photos. Participants here can also be called co-researchers as they take the photographs and engage in the meaning-making with the researchers. This differs fundamentally from traditional research where the power often lies solely with the researcher. Furthermore, the method of photographing enables and encourages participants to be creative and to reflect on the topic.

Photography and other art forms such as drawing, poetry and other visual arts can promote new ideas as they promote stories and a rich weaving of meaning while strengthening relationships. Capturing the sentiment of what is happening in a given community or organization through creative and artistic expression can be experienced as quite different from collecting the same information through surveys, questionnaires, and Likert scales. These innovative research tools invite broader participation that is likely to result in collaboratively achieved transformation.

Six Thinking Hats

This tool employs role-play. Role-play tools encourage participants to move beyond what appears rational (in their attempts to solve the problem) and, instead, play with the topic. The playful moments contribute to the expansion and creation of meanings. The Six Thinking Hats tool invites participants to wear different "hats" as a metaphor to think about their topic from different angles (De Bono, 1985). Using this method, you can have playful interactions where six different kinds of conversations unfold. Each research participant has the opportunity to wear a different conversational hat, and with that opportunity, each participant can "try on" a variety of angles related to the topic. The researcher presents a question which the participants examine for potentially negative outcomes, positive outcomes, while also exploring the question creatively or emotionally. The white hat is associated with the person always looking at the facts and figures of a situation; the yellow hat is optimistic about the topic, raising all the reasons to have a positive attitude about the question/issue. The red hat is the feeling and intuition hat. The black hat is focused on problems and danger that might emerge. The blue is the hat that shows the bigger picture. Finally, the green hat centers on imagination, envisioning what might become of the topic. Six Thinking Hats generates new and multiple viewpoints, expands understanding, and co-creates useful knowledge vis a vis the topic.

Creative and innovative methods for Data meaning-making

After gathering data, co-creating, and expanding ideas on the research topic, we move to interpret the data and related ideas in order to create a plan. There are many methods that help the researcher to do so. Here we are sharing three:

Idea Napkin, Crazy Eights, and Thematic Analysis.

Idea Napkin

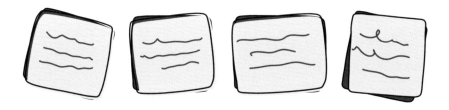

Through a more structured approach, you can compare good ideas and align them. The researcher presents the main meanings that were generated on a wall and invites the research participants to choose their favorite. How to do that?

Each participant takes a napkin and writes a pitch about their favorite idea. The purpose is to get people engaged and excited as they need to articulate their description of the idea. The aim is to present what the idea could offer by way of transforming the organization/community. Each research participant reads their ideas and the others can complement if they want. The pitch also includes the target group that would most benefit from the idea and how they would benefit. The pitch, and the conversations that follow, assists in creating more concrete ideas on the topic and possible ways to move forward (solutions).

This method is used in the context of User Experience Design (UX) and it is known as a fast-paced, generative exercise that motivates participants to think broadly about a theme (https://designsprintkit.withgoogle.com). Participants are asked to sketch eight ideas within eight minutes. The short time of the exercise contributes to a flow of ideas since participants cannot over-think in order to complete the eight ideas. This method helps to collect and integrate ideas. It also helps participants decide what is most important for the project.

The researcher gives each participant 8 sticky notes and then sets a timer for eight minutes. All participants must stop sketching when time is up.

As participants read their ideas, some will not be feasible. Others might be repetitive. There are always some ideas that make an inspiring initiation to the task of defining a plan and creating a specific direction. After all participants have shared their ideas, the researcher invites the next Phase which is a vote for the best ideas. Participants, armed with a couple of sticky dots, can vote on their two favorite ideas out of the group.

This UX tool is fertile to data meaning-making. It is a good way to organize and select the ideas gathered in data generation and check with research participants about what makes sense to them and how they would connect the ideas with more concrete approaches to the topic. As the final step, the chosen ideas can be integrated into more refined designs and prototypes to be tested.

Thematic Analysis

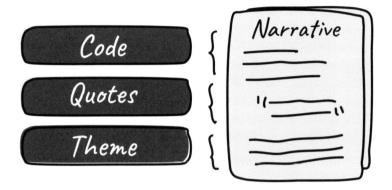

Data meaning-making can also be performed by the researcher alone. Thematic analysis is one method in which the researcher can systematically break data down into meaningful themes (Terry, Hayfield, Clarke & Braun, 2017). If you do not have the time or the availability of the research participants to gather together again in a meaning-making Phase, you can organize your data into themes that will also generate some plans for the prototype.

Before developing themes, it is important to carefully review all the gathered data. As you look over and/or read through the data, you will find that certain topics repeatedly emerge. Create a name (code) for these repeated topics. When you have carefully reviewed all of your data, consider clustering your codes into commonly linked themes. You should then be able to create a coherent story for each theme. Bringing quotes from the text also helps with the coherence or accuracy of the narrative.

Let's look at an example. If you have some data from creative sessions on healthy cooking, you might see that research participants talk a great deal about their experiences adopting a healthier and sustainable style of cooking. They also may talk about the difficulties they experience in making this transition to healthier cooking (e.g., it is more expensive, there is difficulty finding sustainable products, etc.). In addition, some participants might offer tips on how they overcome such challenges. Here you have three codes: experiences with healthy cooking – challenges – opportunities (tips). Choose one color for each code and start highlighting the conversations wherever you recognize the code. Once you have coded all the data, read only the coloured aspects of the transcript from the beginning to the end. Slowly a theme will emerge and a coherent story (narrative) about it. As a final step, look back and check if your themes are still representing your research questions. It is always good to share your codes and themes with others who have fresh eyes. Sometimes, after looking at data for a long period of time, you might miss other elements.

Getting into Prototyping

Now is the moment to take the data meaning-making and begin the process of prototyping. Prototyping is the Phase in design thinking when you quickly test your plan. Prototyping offers the opportunity to bring the ideas to life, experiment, and assess how the environment and the participants feel about the resultant themes.

In Constructionist-Design Research, this is the moment in which we start transforming ideas into action. We examine how the emergent meanings and themes can be activated into tangible plans.

Embracing research as a social process, we want to tap into the potential to transform the community/organization. This is where prototyping can be very helpful for testing possible ways to activate the ideas and meanings that have been generated. In design thinking, prototypes are separated into low- and high-fidelity prototyping.

Low-Fidelity Prototyping

The low-fidelity prototyping means that the idea is translated in a quick and inexpensive way. For example, a low-fidelity prototype for healthy and sustainable cooking could be a paper storyboard inspiring people to shift to a healthy diet. This could take the form of creating a healthy cookbook by using the data on positive experiences, tips, and how to source affordable products. The storyboard can present some variations on how to create and distribute the cookbook and ask participants to offer feedback on each variation. As you can see, this prototype does not require a financial commitment, nor does it require the time and effort needed to create and publish a book before knowing if such a "result" would be useful to the community. With the prototype you have the chance to test, make changes, and improvements.

What are the pros of Low-Fidelity Prototyping? First of all, Low-Fidelity Prototyping is quick and inexpensive. It also provides the opportunity to make instant changes and test new iterations. It also enables the researcher to gain an overview of the idea using minimal time and effort. You can produce simple versions of products in order to test users or canvas the opinions of participants.

What are the cons of Low-Fidelity Prototyping? Because the version of a product/service/experience is basic, it can be devoid of a sense of viability. Furthermore, depending on the details of the experience/product, basic versions might not reflect the nature, appearance, or feel of the finished idea.

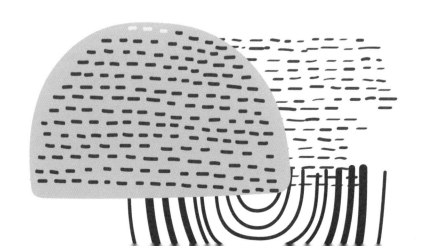

High Fidelity Prototypes

High-fidelity prototypes are those that are more aligned with the finished idea/product. For example, you could create a software system that would support individuals in making the shift to a healthy diet. The software program could allow users to interact with the platform, creating a network and gaining ideas about where to buy products, how to cook, etc. An early version of a software system developed using a design program such as Sketch or Adobe Illustrator is much more time consuming and expensive in comparison to a paper prototype.

What are the pros of High-Fidelity Prototyping? It is engaging as the stakeholders can instantly see their vision realized and will be able to judge how well it meets their expectations, wants, and needs. User testing involving high-fidelity prototypes will allow the evaluators to gather information with a high level of validity and applicability. The closer the prototype is to the finished product, the more confidence the design team will have in how people will respond to, interact with, and perceive the design.

What are the cons of High-Fidelity Prototyping? Different from the low-fidelity prototypes that can be easily changed, making changes to high-fidelity prototypes can take a long time, thus delaying the entire project and sometimes at the cost of losing the original inspiration for the product. In addition, after spending hours of time producing an accurate model with more definitive ideas, there is often less incentive to make changes. Software prototypes may also give test users a false impression of how good the finished product might be.

Due to the pros and cons of low-fidelity and high-fidelity prototyping, it is more common to see low-fidelity prototyping, while high-fidelity prototyping is often used during the later stages, when feedback and evaluations of the experience/product are more refined.

Finalizing with ideas for Experimentation and Implementation

From Data meaning-making to Prototype

The Phase of active ideation and prototyping requires an engaged researcher who is a change agent provoking, collaborating, and inspiring participants. Through the use of creative and innovative design tools (e.g. Storyboard, Photovoice, Crazy Eights, and Thematic Analysis) the researcher curates the generated data, giving meaning to it. The methods help in co-creating new perspectives and ideas, moving toward a tangible plan/solution.

We end the Phase here having transformed traditional data gathering into data generation and transforming data analysis into data meaning-making, opening up the possibility of new and innovative ideas that become a prototype to be experimented and implemented in the next phase.

For our exercise here, if we return to our example of food management, let's imagine that, after data generation and data meaning-making, one possible prototype we refined from data was:

"Shop owners team up with small producers to hire famous local chefs to create a booklet with a variety of recipes that teach people to create meals centered on the 'unused' parts of food. They then host a dinner for the community (small price for attendance)."

This is a possible prototype for experimentation in the next Phase. In the next Chapter, we will unfold this idea.

Before we end this Chapter it is also important, and part of the methodology phase, to consider how we might evaluate the quality of this approach to research. This is especially important if you are conducting academic research and are required to write a report or defend your thesis/dissertation.

How to show the quality of research in this approach?

In the academic research world, it is important to document the quality of the knowledge you are producing. If you are connected to an academic environment and are required to write a research article or a research dissertation/thesis, you cannot escape documenting the rigor and validity of your research. How can we respond to that in a Constructionist-Design Research Framework?

Quality to us is demonstrated in different terms, and in alignment with the values and beliefs of this philosophical approach – the constructionist approach. In Constructionist-Design Research, rigor and validity relate to the resonance of interpretation within a specific community. Reliability concerns the procedure for achieving coherent interpretations within a given community. Rather than aim for replicability or transferability, as one would pursue in classic approaches to research, we center here on the historical and contextual situatedness – that is, the local context in which the knowledge is created. With our attention focused on the resonance and coherence of our "results" for those engaged in the local context of concern, we must reframe several concepts that are tightly associated with traditional research.

From objectivity and neutrality to empathic neutrality

Objectivity refers to the capacity to observe the world without bias. It is to see a world of things that exist apart from human creation. Objectivity demands that the observer remove all subjective and personal elements. However, along with a host of others, we see this as impossible; no one speaks, acts, or observes in a context-free manner.

Objectivity attributed to the scientific method is the result of adopting a certain stance in research. It is an impersonal view of the world which, as we have noted, is impossible to achieve and thus, objective knowledge is also impossible.

We suggest a stance of empathic neutrality. Neutrality means suspending judgment and maintaining an openness toward the actions of all during the data generation and data meaning-making processes. Since no one speaks from "a God's eye view from nowhere," it is impossible for anyone to be objective or neutral. All our actions emerge from value-laden discourse communities. Because we all inhabit different discourse communities, one person's observations may "appear" to be objective but, in fact, they are simply "different." Through empathy, on the other hand, the researcher can express interest and care for the subject.

From generalization to generativity

We are not concerned here with the replicability of the study (showing the validity beyond a single study – empirical truth). Rather, we are concerned with how we might explore and understand the subject of investigation in depth (i.e., we focus on utility and generativity). We recognize that the knowledge produced has local implications - socially situated truths which are context-linked. We look at how useful the research results are for those participating in the context in which the research was conducted. We also consider how we can carefully extend meaning and knowledge produced to new contexts (beyond the single study). Replicability, in the traditional sense, is based on an understanding that the research has uncovered the true answer to the problem being examined. In constructionist research, we look instead for socially situated truths which are context-linked – in other words, local truths.

Rigor as methodological coherence

The methods you choose for your data generation and interpretation must connect with the research questions, demonstrating how your conclusions come from data, etc. Furthermore, transparency of the choices and the steps taken validate the rigor of your research. Providing clarity of your choices invites others to consider how your decisions were made. And, while others may disagree with the choice you have made, if you have coherently articulated your rationale, they can not say you are "wrong."

Thick description

Thick description refers to your detailed description of your approach and procedures, to how you have made choices to select these specific procedures, to how you are proposing your data be generated, and to clearly documenting the process by which you have generated themes, concepts, prototypes. "Thick description refers to the researcher's task of both describing and interpreting observed social action (or behavior) within its particular context" (Ponterotto, 2006, p. 543).

Worldview of the researcher

Here, it is important to make explicit the context from which the researcher has become involved with the project. Is it the researcher's political values, the desire to have a more collaborative environment, a way to get to know a certain community, or something else?

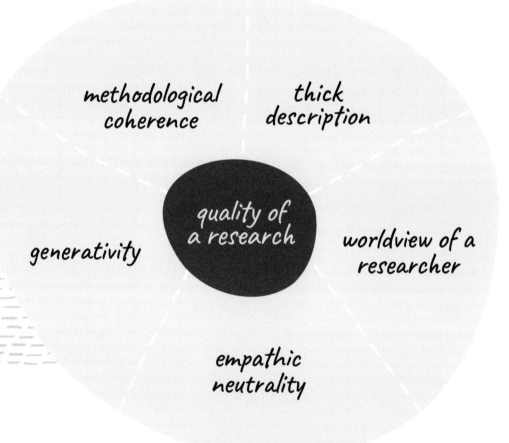

How to guarantee you are making good research decisions?

As you can see, Constructionist-Design Research embraces an approach that differs from a traditional research understanding. Here, the research focus is on the very process of conducting research and how useful it can be for a given context. You can also make use of reflexivity, peer debriefing, and member checking to guarantee that you are on a generative path.

Reflexivity refers to a critical stance in the research process, understanding how the values guiding the research connect to the actions made and considering if other values might be more or less useful. Also to consider are the values of your research participants and how you can be aligned with them. Adopting a reflexive stance takes the form of asking ourselves and others if the assumptions, values, and beliefs we are operating from are the only ones. We are challenged to consider how others might approach the same issue, considering alternative orientations.

Peer debriefing is a process where an "outsider" reviews the data and the analysis. This can be very useful because the "outsider" brings fresh eyes and ears to the project.

Respondent Validation or (member check) refers to sharing the findings with participants for their consideration. This is a way to check the validity of your data.

Final questions for reflection and application to your project:

- Can you describe the difference between data collection and data generation?
- Can you describe the difference between data analysis and data meaning-making?
- What is your favorite creative method and which one is the most useful for your research?
- What are the distinctions between a neutral and objective researcher and a researcher positioned as a change agent?

Experiment and Implement
Forming-futures in Research Phase 4

This chapter will introduce:

- How to experiment with a prototype
- What a platform is and how to create one
- How to use collective creativity, relational responsibility, and imagination in prototype testing
- How to evaluate your prototype in action
- Research as future-forming

Introduction

This chapter introduces the final Phase of the Constructionist-Design Research Framework. In this Phase we are focusing on the initial prototype created in Phase 3, testing it, refining it, and envisioning possible directions. It is about experimenting with opportunities, checking the utility and the practical purpose of the prototype, and from there, reflecting on how that might work, as we prepare for implementation.

This final Phase is the convergence of all prior Phases. It is the by-product of the research process, moving us from the co-construction of the topic, the creation of generative research questions, and the design of data creation methods, to the development of a plan (prototype). Now it is time to Experiment and Implement.

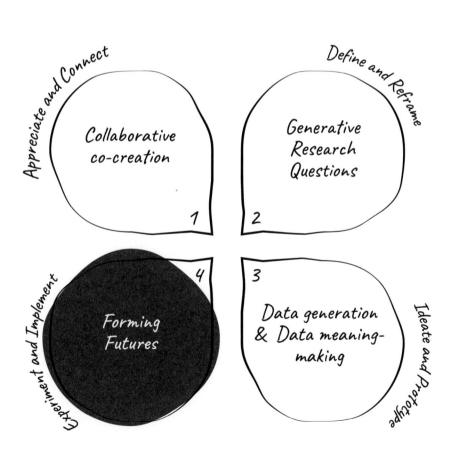

Experimenting with the prototype

Traditional research experimentation is about testing the instrumental and empirical validity of the study findings. Many designers/researchers work with experimentation in technical and representational ways, discussing data, separating variables, establishing cause and effect, and discussing best practices to assist in deciding on the implementation processes.

Constructionist-Design Research Experimentation is about experimenting in a dynamic and fluid way, focusing on the utility and relevance of data within a certain context and with certain people.

Here, we understand experimentation as a performance (Pickering, 2013). As we experiment, we perform new actions and therefore unfold new possibilities, new worlds. We focus here on how ideas (prototypes) connect, interact, and move together when activated.

We work with the research findings not with an interest in how they "fit the world," but how they will "act to create a world."

This is coherent with the constructionist notion that research is a social practice that is future-forming. Thus, findings are not representational but constructive, generating the potential for new creations.

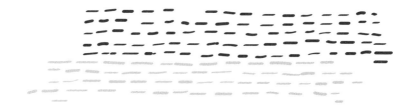

The Constructionist-Design Phase 4 connects the findings with the local context and the people in a performative manner. According to Pickering (2013), data is not simply cognitive information. Data is also a performance upon which you can act by experimenting. Pickering talks about the elements that play a role in an environment - people, places, spaces, things - as agencies dancing together creating new configurations. They don't interact in a cause and effect way but organically and dynamically, creating possible combinations and realities. **Pickering (2022) calls this experimentational performance a dance of agency**.

By experimenting, you open the way for this interactive dance and are able to see how the interaction of all elements will unfold in solutions (good or bad). With this process you see various possibilities of going on together and with that you can make more informed decisions on the final implementation.

How can you initiate this dance for purposes of designing a successful experimentation?

Throughout the Phases, we have been exploring the issue of food management. Let's explore this process using it once again to see how experimentation and implementation might look in action.

The food management System - the issue of food waste

This is a relevant and complex topic with a network of social actors involved, making up a vast supply chain. The system is unsustainable, and it contributes to environmental damage, biodiversity loss, as well as inequality of distributions. How can we create long-term economic and societal resilience and guarantee a sustainable food system? As you can see, many directions for research are possible and relevant. How might we address this issue?

With the Constructionist-Design approach, as mentioned earlier, we start by moving away from simple questions such as "What is wrong?" "How do you deal with the problem of food waste here?" "Why is this causing disputes concerning small farms and habits of consumption?" An analysis oriented by these questions would create a focus and direction on the negative side of the "problem" – the food waste and how to fix it. Instead, we started from an appreciative approach in Design Phase 1.

In the *Design Phase 1 - Appreciating and Connecting: Collaborative co-creation* - we started with a review of literature as well as conversations with people involved in food production and distribution: supermarkets, consumers, and other distribution channels.

With that, we expanded our learning about what is central, how production is unsustainable, and how distribution is unequal. We also reversed our questions and asked, "are there sustainable productions?" "where is distribution equal?" Through collaborative co-creation, we discussed how to shift from the traditional research approach, related to a lack of food, unsustainable production, and faulty distribution, to an appreciative approach where the focus could be placed on what gives life to the system, what works well in this system. As a consequence, our attention is centered on possibilities. The first Phase ended with a more complex understanding of the topic, with an appreciative approach. In addition, we always end the first Phase with a map of the system that allows us to see the complexity and interconnections of all the themes and people related to the topic.

As an example, if we create a rhizomatic map featuring the outcome of Design Phase 1, we might have something like this:

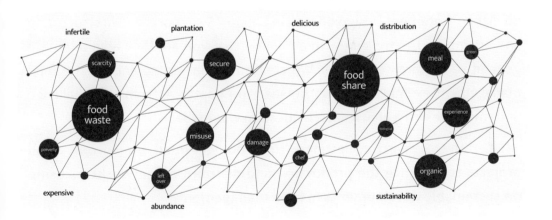

Having mapped the system, in *Design Phase 2 - Define and Reframe: Generative Research Questions* - we then fine-tuned the theme for the research process by creating the generative research question(s). To do so, we framed and reframed the ideas about food management in an attempt to generate research questions.

In the framing and reframing process, we moved from food waste to food sharing as our starting point.

As we saw, the underlying principle of the reframe is that food belongs to all of us and thus we start from the perspective of sharing.

Food waste calls for a more individualistic, rational, and hierarchical attitude to solve the problem. Food sharing, as opposed to food waste, involves the whole system and everyone.

We can share production and distribution. With this new framing, the issue also shifts from an attempt to fix a problem to a focus on the ways in which the topic is central for all of us, thereby underscoring our responsibility and involvement. Once we shift from a problem orientation to an appreciative orientation, and frame and reframe the topic, we are ready to formulate the generative questions.

To help in the articulation of the results from these first two Phases, the Challenge Statement Design offered in Chapter 3 supports you in structuring and organizing the topic in such a manner that you are then able to design generative research questions. We created a final statement for the food management example that can be seen in Chapter 4. From the Challenge Statement Design a final research question was made:

Generative Research Question: **"How do we build on current food projects to enhance the production and distribution networks focusing on sustainable developments in food management?"**

Equipped with the generative research question we moved then to *Design Phase 3 - Ideate and Prototype: Data generation & Data meaning-making* - focused on methodology. Here, we are concerned with engaging the social actors involved in the research so that, together, we can embark on a search for meaning.

Based on the generative research question above, you can think of your participants as consumers, farmers, and organizations already working with the concept of food sharing, collaborative processes, and sustainability.

Continuing the exercise, let's recall two design tools offered in Design Phase 3 to briefly show how to conduct data generation and data meaning-making.

Design Tool Data Generation: Storyboard (recall)

Storyboard is a simple yet creative way to generate data on a topic. Here you can organize a creative session with around eight research participants from different perspectives and sides of the food chain. The researcher presents the topic inspired by the generative research question and poses a question to the group. The question should not be exactly the same as the research question since the research question is typically quite formal, used to guide the direction of the research. Here, you can frame a more creative question such as: "What is your experience of sustainably sharing food?" "Tell us a story of collaboration in the food chain?"

Each participant writes on a piece of paper or sticky note their story. After that, all the stories are posted on the wall (or any other surface that is available where all participants can see and can add their responses). The researcher invites participants to read all of the stories and offer ideas of possible similarities or combinations. The group slowly develops a collective story of the topic, exploring it in a visual and narrative format. The process of talking and negotiating combinations of stories is an illustration of meaning creation and meaning-making.

Examples of stories could be:

Consumer 1:

My most sustainable story of sharing food was when I had the opportunity to buy from a shop where I knew the origin of the food. I knew it was from a farmer who grew everything organically.

Consumer 2:

My most sustainable story was participating in an initiative called "Bring Out the Best" where people were asked to gather leftovers from their refrigerator and a famous chef would transform them into meals.

Farmer:

My most sustainable story of sharing food was to gain support from local supermarkets to have the guarantee that my organic production would be sold to them.

Supermarket owner:

My most sustainable story of sharing food was an experiment where we embraced 'ugly' vegetables so that edible food would not go uneaten simply due to appearance. The farmers could deliver the "ugly-looking" food, thereby not wasting it, and the consumers could buy less expensive vegetables and fruit, saving food that would have otherwise gone to waste.

With each successful story and the unfolding dialogue around their experiences, meanings emerge and one collective narrative is built: The idea of a powerful network where stakeholders are valuing local food resources. Producers of organic products are empowered with the assurance that their farm products will be acquired. Shop owners and distributors promote the direct acquisition of food from the producer. Consumers become directly involved in the process and have knowledge and a voice, thereby having the ability to participate in the process.

Here we are illustrating the exercise with one design tool. However, in your project, you can and should add more creative sessions to gather more data before moving to data meaning-making. For the sake of this exercise, we will move directly to the analysis. Now, with the collective narrative, you can move to create your prototype. For this, we can use some tools from data meaning-making. Let's practice the crazy eights.

Design Tool Data Meaning-Making: Crazy eights (recall)

Here, you can use the participants who worked with you on the Storyboard or you could invite new participants. What is important is that you continue the process of moving data generation into data meaning-making. Gather together all the data and share with the participants the possible narratives created. Ask them to think of some possible ways to move forward (solutions). In this specific design tool, participants will sketch eight ideas within eight minutes. The short time of the exercise contributes to a free flow of ideas, preventing too much rational thinking and encouraging more free thinking.

Each participant will envision solutions, which they then share among themselves and give feedback to each other. The researcher facilitates the exchanges, co-creating the combination of the most powerful, yet feasible, idea to prototype.

Many ideas emerge, culminating in inspiring experiences and projects that alert people to the topic, offering ways for them to participate, and slowly make the change. As the final step, the chosen ideas will be integrated into more refined designs and prototypes to be tested.

For our exercise here, let's imagine one possible prototype to be tested that can be formed from the data generation and data meaning-making:

"Shop owners team up with small producers to hire famous local chefs to create a booklet with a variety of recipes that teach people to create meals centered on the 'unused' parts of food. They then host a dinner for the community (small price for attendance)".

We are now ready for *Design Phase 4 - Experiment and Implement: Forming Futures*. It is time to experiment with what has been created and open to a larger audience.

Experimenting with the prototype created

The prototype to be tested in this specific case might be the creation of a network of stakeholders involved with food culminating with an event: dinner for the community. The Experiment follows three steps: *Creation of a Platform – Application of Collective Creativity & Relational Responsibility - Stimulation of Imagination.*

 *Creation of a platform*

The first step is the creation of the Platform to enable the performance of the agencies - the people, places, spaces and all things involved in the experiment (Pickering, 2013). The performance is the interactive dance of all these elements in the prototype. The platform is the necessary space to provide that.

A platform is described as an interactive environment (online or offline), for interlinked stakeholders, where co-creation is enabled with value creation as the main objective (van Dam, 2019). The platform will be the stage for the performance of the prototype to be enacted.

A platform sets the stage for collective creativity to take place and new configurations to emerge. Starting with your prototype, design an environment that invites participation in order to perform the idea and to create conditions for evaluation and final Implementation. The interactive dance of the elements will be supported by the platform. Each project will require a different platform to support the idea to be activated.

It is important that this platform is designed as an open system so that multiple social actors can participate and interact in different formats. As a researcher, you need to be attentive to what type of platform you will create. For our prototype here, the platform should be offline, to support the encounter of all stakeholders to co-create the event: a dinner for the community.

Pickering talks about two aspects of this performance/dance to which you should pay attention: decentralized and emergent. The performance is decentralized because no one should have control over the process and emergent in the sense that the process should play the most important role revealing how things might work in the unfolding interactions. In this way, this dance will be truly creative and useful.

Action:

The platform makes the Experiment tangible. You must think of who will participate, where activities will happen, what the event will be named, and dates.

The platform can be a place within a certain community where the final event will take place. The researcher can propose the creation of a team where shop owners, small producers-farmers, chefs, and community come together to discuss what they have in mind for the dinner and what their responsibilities would be. Identify two people from each side: two farmers; two shop owners; two chefs and two community members. Identify a place for the meeting in the community that can also be the event location, perhaps the neighborhood community center to attract more locals. Create a name for the project and schedule a date and time for the meeting and a final day for the event.

For our example here let's say that the team decided on one meeting per week for 2 months and on the 3rd month, the event will take place. The event will be called **"Fresh to Share."**

Application of Collective Creativity & Relational Responsibility

Collective creativity and relational responsibility assist in co-creating new forms of engagements and working processes. They also help us understand if the prototype is working from a collective perspective, thereby making it possible to move coherently and accordingly and, if people are willing to commit together, to move forward to implementation.

Collective creativity will arise from the interaction of the ideas of diverse people rather than from the separate individuals. In collective creativity we free ourselves from judgments to combine and interconnect ideas and frame them into possible new actions. Collective Creativity refers to the capacity to be curious in relation to ideas in order to explore possibilities that go beyond what is given (the data), thereby generating innovative thoughts.

Relational Responsibility is the process in which individuals together take responsibility for what is created. McNamee and Gergen (1999) introduce the idea of a relational process that replaces the individual as the central concern. In that way, the notion of relational responsibility moves away from the idea of individuals being independent and autonomous, instead focusing on the collective process of building engagement, a sense of belonging and co-responsibility for the projects.

Action:

Set up the once-a-week meetings to have space for all to talk. Let people experience the prototype as they engage with the proposal. Ask initial questions to the farmers about how they would guarantee the freshness of the food and how they might transport the food to the event location.

Ask the chefs:

What can they cook? How they can adapt to what is seasonally available?

Supermarket owners:

How do they imagine working in partnership with the farmers?

Community:

How might they engage the community to participate? What would be an appealing invitation to the event?

Ask all participants for their own experiences and invite others to build upon the ideas. That is when collective creativity is triggered. When many participants voice their views and ideas on a topic, the potential to create meaningful experiences is amplified. As a consequence, relational responsibility will be built as common ground is established, allowing the group to move forward together. At the end, ask follow up-questions to make sure everyone is aligned and ready for the next meeting. Each meeting will build upon the previous one, producing more concrete ideas about how to create the event.

Stimulation of Imagination

Imagination is the human capacity to create something that does not yet exist. Imagination releases us from boundaries, encourages creativity, spontaneity, and novelty. Imagination in research is the act of moving beyond the already established to start envisioning new combinations of ideas (Camargo-Borges, 2018). Meanings form new images and scenarios never before thought.

By imagining these scenarios of a prototype, we open the opportunity to bring the ideas into reality.

In the process of experimenting a prototype, imagination is increased by collective creativity. Inviting the collective imagination favors future possibilities and great potential for future implementation.

How can we apply imagination in the food management project?

Action:

Once you have an alignment of ideas discussed by all stakeholders, the next task is to look at all information and stories created on the platform. Here we draw upon the collective creativity of the group and start imagining what the event will look like. Invite participants to look at the proposed activity with an open mind and imagine everything, from decoration to how the message of food sharing and sustainability will be passed to all guests.

For this project, **"Fresh to Share"**, we could offer a dinner with sustainable products and a menu created with recipes from family traditions within the community. The creators of the family recipes would be identified and shared on the menu. The tables would be set having a diversity of people sharing dinner, able to talk together, get to know each other, and share ideas. For each course of the meal, one question (related to participants' experiences and ideas for moving forward) would be asked. The table participants would share their opinions and write some ideas down on a piece of paper. Each table would be sampling a different menu, allowing for a comparative test of the public's acceptance. The community would be asked, at the end of the meal, to share their impressions. After the **"Fresh to Share"** event, a book containing the recipes that the community rated as successes would be created, including the participants' ideas and opinions. The book could be sold for a small price, with all proceeds allocated to fund future events to further advance the theme of food sharing.

The following chart supports you in experimenting with your Prototype by moving from data into action.

Constructionist-Design Research Phase 4
From Data Meaning-Making to Experiment with the Prototype

What	How
Prototype	*Describe your prototype here*
Creation of **a Platform – the platform makes the experiment tangible.**	Write down who will participate; where and how the activities will transpire; and dates.
Application of **Collective Creativity & Relational Responsibility – co-creating new forms of engagements and working processes.**	Describe how the environment will be created and what questions will trigger creative and engaging experiences.
Stimulation of **Imagination – triggering new ideas and expanding possibilities in the experiment**	Look at the activities and write down evocative questions and propositions that invite the expansion of the ideas and the experiment.

From Experimentation to Implementation

How do you know when an experiment is ready to be implemented as a permanent action? An experiment is not always a success at first and sometimes will not go well in the first go-round. That means you might have to run a couple of experiments, embracing the learning and reflections from the previous one. van Dam (2019) offers a model to evaluate the prototype that can support you in realizing what is working well and what should change. It can also help insure it is going in desirable directions. The model is called ACTIVE (van Dam and Ouwens, 2016) and can be used as a starting point for evaluating an experiment. The letters ACTIVE stand for: Appreciative, Co-creative, Transformative, Imaginative, Values-based, and Experience-focused. With ACTIVE, you can pose questions and fine-tune. Active also is useful in generating conversations with all involved in the Experiment include bringing together all perspectives and experiences.

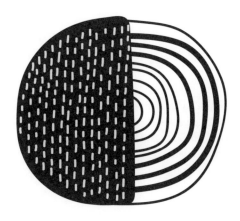

ACTIVE Model
Question: Does or did the Platform...

Appreciative
- use positive language and images?
- build upon the strengths, energy, and potential instead of the problems and impossibilities?
- create new inspiring perspectives for the future?

Co-creative
- build upon the power of the stakeholders?
- keep the dialogue open and alive, catalyzing interactions?
- let the involved stakeholders create/design themselves or invite them to create themselves?

Transformative
- focus on desired change?
- inspire people to think or act differently?
- lead to a sustainable, desired, and valuable change or future?

Imaginative
- appeal to the imagination of stakeholders?
- consciously use creativity or invite stakeholders to use creativity?
- create or trigger new ideas or combinations that don't exist yet?

Values-based
- work from (shared) values?
- reflect or make visible which (shared) values are used?
- add meaning for stakeholders?

Experience-focused
- inspire participation?
- evoke positive emotions? (for example by the design of the platform: look and feel, colours, the way they trigger the senses, storyline etc.)
- create a long-lasting impression and resonate with stakeholders?

Van Dam, 2019

After having evaluated the event by answering the questions from ACTIVE, it is also important to ask these questions: Is this event desirable from the perspective of all involved? Is continuity of this event feasible? Does this event offer viable solutions to food management and the creation of sustainable networks of production and distribution? Desirability, feasibility, and viability are also crucial elements to make decision to move from Experiment to Implement.

Future-Forming: Unfolding New Worlds

As you can see, the Constructionist-Design Research Framework looks at data as a construction and at experiment as a performance. Researchers, along with the research participants, use this opportunity to build connection and engagement among ideas, thereby creating co-responsibility for the idea/action to be implemented. That means, the Experimentation and Implementation Phase will build upon the constructed data and perform it, forming futures, unfolding new worlds.

Unfolding new worlds here means that, by igniting the process of experimenting with the ideas in a more tangible way, new possibilities will emerge presenting us with new forms of action, new behavior, new realities, new worlds.

This matches well with the concept of research as future-forming (Gergen, 2014). In future-forming research, the aim is to change existing situations into preferred ones. It is not about looking at what "is there," but about creating new forms of action, thereby creating alternative possibilities for society, organizations, and communities.

Thus, as we saw, experimentation is not about simply testing the prototype and implementing it somewhere. We need a platform, collective creativity & relational responsibility, and imagination to provoke participation and to envision the creation of something new. Experimentation will engage all the elements for emergence. That will enable us to visualize the best way to move forward.

We hope that through the example of food management you can have a better sense of how each Phase unfolds in what becomes the prototype and how the experimentation generates new possibilities for implementation.

Final questions for reflection and application to your project:

- How would you create an environment for experimentation?
- Is the ACTIVE model useful for evaluating your prototype?
- How can you design research that is future-forming and can unfold futures?

Research as Intervention
Transcending Dichotomies

This chapter will introduce:

- The relevance of research as creative, engaging, and innovative
- The importance of transcending dichotomies in research
- The power of research as future-forming
- Ethics in relational research
- The powerful unity of social construction and design thinking
- The core positions of a researcher in this Research Framework

Transcending dichotomies – The relevance of creative and innovative research

When we think of research, we are most commonly invited into the tradition that emerged in an historical moment where progress, stability, uniformity, and singular solutions met the demands of the moment. This tradition would also invite us to see research either as quantitative or qualitative. However, we live in a different, complex world today. While the world has always been complex, multiple, and chaotic, our ability today to be instantly interconnected and globally aware increases the need for research approaches that embrace our multiplicity and our chaotic ways of living. We live in a moment that acknowledges the diversity of worldviews and lifestyles.

The present world requires approaches to research that subvert and transcend dichotomies and tap into diversity, connection and interdependencies, avoiding the search for a singular, "right" answer. The present world requires that researchers embrace forms of knowledge and wisdom that move beyond our academic rigidity, recognizing that the communities, cultures, and issues that researchers are examining require – in order to be useful – working with creative, engaging, and inclusive methodologies. In other words, researchers must learn from and with those communities, organizations, and institutions that are seeking transformation.

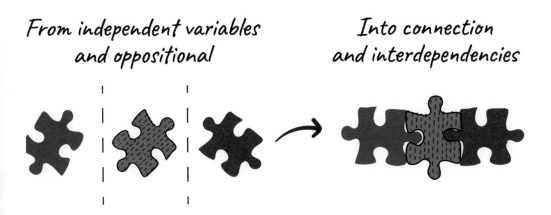

From independent variables and oppositional

Into connection and interdependencies

New movements in research invite us to rethink, problematize, and transcend dichotomies that are rooted in the social sciences such as the polarizations between *research and intervention, science and society, and thinking and doing.*

Research and Intervention

Traditionally, as we have mentioned, research is viewed as a process of discovery – a discovery of what is "out there" in the world, already existing. Such a view of research is blind to the influences and effects of the researcher and the researcher's questions, methods, and analyses. As we hope we have made clear, our very presence as researchers affect and impact the systems we investigate. The questions we ask emerge from the communities of which we are a part (the academic; the professional; the cultural). For example, a medical practitioner is more likely to ask questions about how your body works than questions concerning your emotions about your body. Questions, methods, and modes of analysis are not neutral; nor are researchers neutral. Thus, research is not a process of discovering what already exists. It is a process of constructing a way of understanding (i.e., constructing meaning/knowledge). To that end, all research is transformative and future-forming. We intervene and create change in the very process of research.

Thus, we emphasize here research and intervention; not research or intervention. We call attention to the importance of the researcher and the process of conducting research, which includes the choices we make and the methods we select. In this way, we see the researcher as a change agent and the methodologies we use as creative, interactive, and engaging.

Furthermore, as Kuhn (1962) demonstrated, scientific research is also a process of construction. Different communities of scientists make different assumptions that lead to different research approaches and, as a consequence, different ways to formulate research questions, methods, analyses, and – consequently – conclusions. Varying scientific communities make sense of data in ways that often invite a shift in paradigm. For example, Copernicus revolutionized our view of the cosmos by describing the sun, rather than the earth, as the center of the universe. This paradigm shift changed the role of astronomy. But in addition to acknowledging that scientific communities are also in the business of constructing knowledge, we must consider the largest distinction between the natural sciences and the social sciences. In the social sciences, we are working with people – people who live in language, have imaginative capabilities, and can create and reflect on their understandings of the world. These abilities provide us all with the opportunity to create what does not yet exist, change decisions, act in unpredictable ways, and enter into relations that provide us with alternative views. As you have seen throughout this book, we take advantage of such abilities to work with science and society together, co-creating more desirable futures. The emphasis here is that Science and Society are not in opposition but belong together, influencing each other and changing each other as they evolve/unfold.

Thinking and Doing

The scientific tradition of research has claimed isolated elements as the unit of analysis. This has translated, largely, into a focus on the individual as independent, the source of praise or blame, at the expense of examining interactive processes taking place within entire ecosystems. The focus on the individual as someone who acts in an independent world, ignores the interconnections of the system and individuals as inescapable participants. It dismisses what people do together and co-create with their environment.

In a similar fashion, isolating thinking from doing treats each activity as independent. We view thinking and doing as intricately interconnected. To the constructionist, thinking is an activity. We refer to it as inner dialogue that is populated by the voices of others. In this regard, like doing, we are actively engaging as we think – thinking is no longer viewed as a private act. And, it is impossible to separate thinking and doing; the ways in which we make meaning (think) give birth to particular forms of doing. In the same way, what we do in interaction informs our inner dialogue.

The Constructionist-Design Research Framework, unlike our inherited research tradition, places emphasis on (1) the ways in which our research creates change (i.e., serves as an intervention), (2) takes seriously the relational, interconnected, unfolding nature of human/social life, and (3) acknowledges interactive processes as the locus of meaning construction. Embracing these foci can provoke creative and innovative ways to conduct research, identifying research as a form of social transformation. The traditional division between theory/research (discovery) and practice/consulting (change) is erased, suggesting that we can view any sort of consultancy (i.e., organizations, education, healthcare, even therapy, etc.) as a form of research. We hope that this image is liberating, allowing you to see yourself as a researcher/change agent.

To us, the integration of social construction and design thinking embraces the demands of the complex social world in which we live. We have the ability to reflect on our actions and choices. We have the ability to inspire and become inspired, to imagine, to create and recreate, to frame and reframe, redefining our understandings and our ways of thinking and doing. We have access to multiple and (often) competing worldviews. Such diversity and complexity require methods that allow for the multivocality amongst which we live. If we are to survive in a social world of diversity, we must find ways of examining (and co-creating) social life that celebrates difference and avoids outcomes that perpetuate divisiveness.

The Power of Future-Forming Research

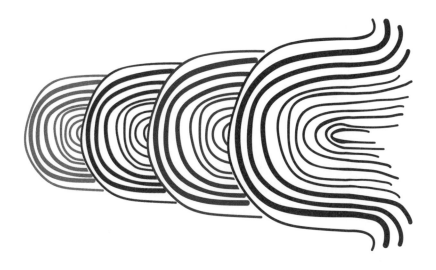

The Constructionist-Design Research Framework that we have presented in this book focuses on research as future-forming, as action, developed through creative and imaginative, emergent processes that involve a community of people constructing and reconstructing knowledge and practice together. Considering the role of designers as co-creators of knowledge and co-creators of transformational possibilities, social construction offers an invitation to researchers to become practitioner-researchers; that is, researchers of everyday life. This stance towards research sees knowledge as constructed, as a coordination of a collective process of collaboration among the participants in a system. Research, in this approach, is very much process oriented. The openness to the innovative methods used and the sensitivity to the context require and allow a creative attitude for the Constructionist-Design Researcher.

The Constructionist-Design Research Framework liberates the researcher (and participants) from the constraints of realism (Camargo-Borges & Gergen, 2022), engaging in creativity as the key to form innovative futures (Montuori & Donnelly, 2020).

When we understand meanings and actions as constructions – that is, byproducts of participants' engagements with each other and their environment – we avoid taking our understandings of the world for granted. Whatever the problem is, it can be reframed.

This also invites creativity and imagination into the activity of research. If we are not bound by those taken for granted realities and logics, then we can use imagination in our research process, creating and recreating our social lives, unfolding new worlds.

Here, we also challenge the narrative of progress that is so strong in science (McNamee & Hoskings, 2012). The idea of progress has many dimensions but, most often in research, it is understood as a steady movement towards improved developments and advances. The understanding is that science works in a cumulative way, metaphorically putting one brick on top of another to build the wall. Science adds one result to another to ultimately answer all the problems of the social world. Despite the contribution that knowledge and new actions bring to the world, here we invite a view of a generative process of creating knowledge, and not a cumulative one. Research brings a process of continuity and enrichment where people together co-create their place, space, and society.

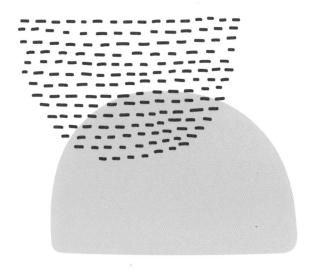

The Ethics of Research

If a researcher is not neutral and objective as we have discussed, then s/he should always be intentional and always act in a way that opens alternatives. Heinz von Foerster (1993) calls this the ethical imperative: Act always so as to increase your options. This is also how the Constructionist-Design Research Framework evolves. The aim is to be a creative catalyst, to support the emergence of choices. This is an ethical position that enables the transformation of challenging situations into more desirable ones.

McNamee (2015) suggests that the relational, processual focus of social construction shifts our understanding of ethics from a universal, codified sense of ethics (as in an ethical code that all follow) to an ethic of discursive potential. An ethic of discursive potential positions the researcher in that very stance of exploring alternatives – literally expanding our ways of talking about and giving meaning to our topic. We see this in Phase 2 where, in an attempt to craft a generative research question, we engage in processes of framing and reframing the collaboratively co-created visions of the research topic – visions that have emerged from the appreciative stance taken by the researcher and participants in Phase 1. This ethic of discursive potential meets the ethical imperative of respecting the context, the people, and expanding options.

As a researcher working within the Constructionist-Design Research Framework, your task is not only one of working collaboratively with participants to create new futures but to build an environment where diverse and multiple voices can be heard and respected. Clearly, this captures a relationally sensitive ethic and avoids imposition of an ethic of right/wrong. This ethic invites the researcher to interact, understand, and co-construct meanings that generate ethical decisions and future actions. It acknowledges the centrality of all participants' meanings and understandings, including one's own.

The Powerful Unity of Social Construction and Design Thinking

It might be useful to return to the basic assumptions and features of social construction and the central concepts and principles of design thinking.

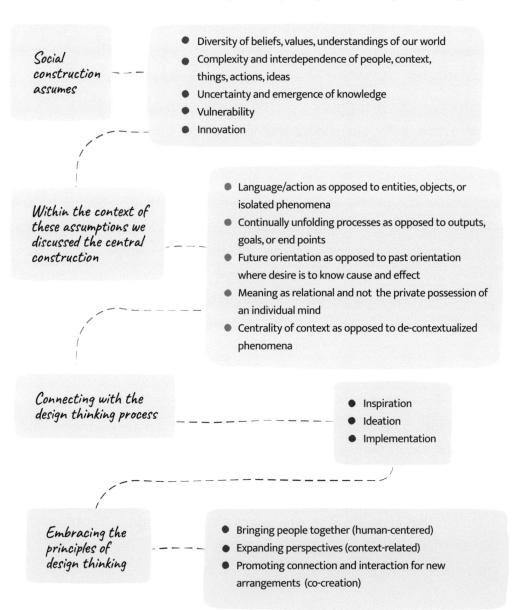

Social construction assumes
- Diversity of beliefs, values, understandings of our world
- Complexity and interdependence of people, context, things, actions, ideas
- Uncertainty and emergence of knowledge
- Vulnerability
- Innovation

Within the context of these assumptions we discussed the central construction
- Language/action as opposed to entities, objects, or isolated phenomena
- Continually unfolding processes as opposed to outputs, goals, or end points
- Future orientation as opposed to past orientation where desire is to know cause and effect
- Meaning as relational and not the private possession of an individual mind
- Centrality of context as opposed to de-contextualized phenomena

Connecting with the design thinking process
- Inspiration
- Ideation
- Implementation

Embracing the principles of design thinking
- Bringing people together (human-centered)
- Expanding perspectives (context-related)
- Promoting connection and interaction for new arrangements (co-creation)

As we have attempted to make clear throughout this book, the marriage of social construction, as the philosophical perspective, and design thinking, as the practical perspective, offer us a view of research as a dynamic, continually unfolding process of co-creation. It positions research as an endeavor that forges futures. It positions researchers as change agents.

Together, social construction and design thinking privilege the criterion of utility over veracity. In other words, unlike traditional research where truth (veracity) is assumed to be the ultimate criterion, in the Constructionist-Design Research Framework we ask if the byproduct – the outcome – of our research is useful. Who is it useful for? In what context? And at what historical moment. There is no illusion that what serves as a generative way to form a future for one community, organization, or context will be generative for another. And, importantly, there is no illusion that the researcher knows best what is generative for a given research context and its participants. Participants must be part of the choices and decisions that emerge.

This means that, within the Framework we have introduced here, all research is viewed as a process of construction. To that end, all research is transformative. As we move through the four Phases of the Constructionist-Design Framework, we note that each Phase involves action, creativity, involvement, and collaboration. We leave behind the image of the lone researcher solving the problems of the world.

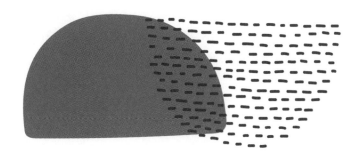

The researcher is at the center of igniting all these processes and we conclude here with a blueprint of the abilities/positions/attributes you hold as a researcher. We have emphasized different qualities Phase by Phase, connected to the Research Framework, however they can be embraced throughout the entire research process.

The Constructionist-Design Researcher in Action

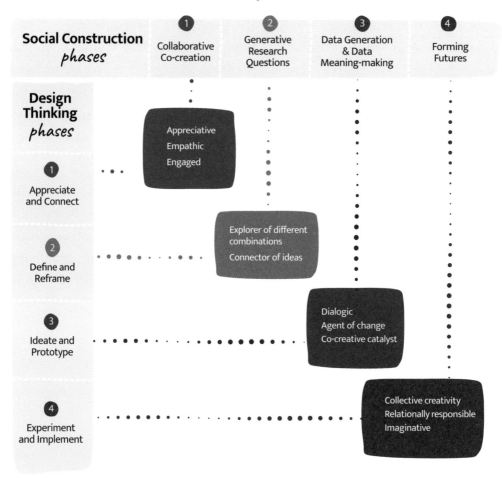

Creating New Futures, Unfolding New Worlds

When design thinking and social construction are embraced, there is a generative quality with the aim of being useful to the context in which it emerges. Additionally, there is an ability to produce new processes and issues that assist us in evaluating knowledge. An openness to the methods used and a sensitivity to the context require and allow a creative attitude of the Constructionist-Design Researcher. This design approach to research challenges universal knowledge and its inclination to predict and control, instead inviting a closer look at local knowledge, at different voices and perspectives, and at the dynamics of our ever-changing world/society. If knowledge is co-created in relationship, in context, and in history, this approach to research invites not only an understanding of this creation but also a recreation of new forms of knowledge, creating new futures, and unfolding new worlds.

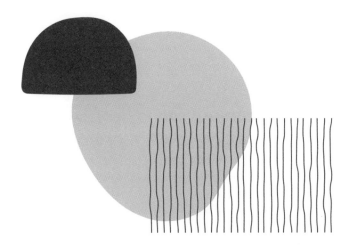

Final questions for reflection and application to your project:

- How can you become an appreciative and dialogic researcher?
- How can you reconcile research and intervention? Science and research? Thinking and doing?
- Can you describe the relevance of combining social construction and design thinking?

References

Bakhtin, M. (1981). *The dialogic imagination: four essays.* University of Texas Press.

Banathy, B. H. (1996). *Designing social systems in a changing world.* Plenum Press.

Bateson, G. (1980). *Mind and nature: a necessary unity.* Fontana/Collins.

Benford, R. D., & Snow, D. A. (2000). Framing processes and social movements: an overview and assessment. *Annual review of sociology*, 26, 611-639. DOI: https://doi:10.1146/annurev.soc.26.1.611.

Bissola, R., Imperatori, B., & Biffi, A. (2017). A rhizomatic learning process to create collective knowledge in entrepreneurship education: Open innovation and collaboration beyond boundaries. *Management learning*, 48(2), 206–226. DOI: https://doi.org/10.1177/1350507616672735.

Bodiford, K. & Camargo-Borges, C. (2014). Bridging research and practice: illustrations from appreciative inquiry in doctoral research. *AI practitioner journal (International journal of appreciative inquiry)*, 16 (3). DOI: dx.doi.org/10.12781/978-1-907549-20-5.

Brown, T. (2009). *Change by design: how design thinking transforms organizations and inspires innovation.* Harper Collins.

Brown, T., & Wyatt, J. (2010). *Design thinking for social innovation.* Stanford social innovation review. DOI: https://doi.org/10.1596/1020-797X_12_1_29.

Burr, V. (2015). *Social constructionism.* (3rd Edition). Routledge.

Camargo-Borges, C., & Rasera, E. F. (2013). Social constructionism in the context of organization development: dialogue, imagination, and co-creation as resources of change. *SAGE Open.* DOI: https://doi.org/10.1177/2158244013487540.

Camargo-Borges, C. (2017). Creativity and imagination: research as world making!. In Leavy, P., *Handbook of arts-based research* (pp. 88-100). Guilford Press.

Camargo-Borges, C. (2019). A-ppreciating: How to discover the generative core. In Nijs, D. (Ed.), *Advanced imagineering: designing innovation as collective creation* (pp. 90-104). Edward Elgar Publisher.

Camargo-Borges, C. & Gergen, K. (2022). Social construction and the forming of futures. In Montuori, A. & Donnelly, G. (Ed.). *The handbook for creative futures.* Taylor & Francis/Routledge.

Cooperrider, D. L., & Whitney, D. (2005). Appreciative inquiry: a positive revolution in change. Berrett-Koehler Publishers.

Corning, P. A (2012). *The re-emergence of emergence, and the causal role of synergy in emergent evolution.* Synthese, 185 (2), 295–317. Retrieved 30 june 2022, from http://www.jstor.org/stable/41477699.

Creswell, J. (2007). *Qualitative inquiry and research design.* (2nd ed.). SAGE Publications.

Cross, N. (2006). *Designerly ways of knowing.* Springer.

Czarniawska, B. (2004). *Narratives in social science research: introducing qualitative methods.* SAGE Publications.

De Bono, E. (1985). *Six thinking hats: an essential approach to business management.* Little, Brown, & Company.

Design sprints. (n.d.). *Share and engage with the design sprints.* Retrieved 30 June 2022, from https://designsprintkit.withgoogle.com/.

Deleuze, G., & Guattari, F. (2013). *A thousand plateaus.* Bloomsbury Academic.

Entman, R. M. (1993). Framing: toward clarification of a fractured paradigm. *Journal of communication,* 43(4), 51–58. DOI: https://doi.org/10.1111/j.1460-2466.1993.tb01304.x.

Foerster, H. V. (1993). *KybernEthik.* Merve Verlag.

Foucault, M. (1972). *The archaeology of knowledge and the discourse on language.* Pantheon Books.

Geertz, C. (1973). *The interpretation of culture.* Basic Books.

Gergen, K. J. (1978). Toward generative theory. *Journal of personality and social psychology,* 36 (11), 1344-1360. DOI: https://doi.org/10.1037/0022-3514.36.11.1344.

Gergen, K. J. (1994). *Realities and relationships: soundings in social construction.* Harvard University Press.

Gergen, K. J., McNamee, S., & Barrett, F. (2001). Toward transformative dialogue. *International journal of public administration,* 24 (7), 697-707. DOI: https://doi.org/10.1081/PAD-100104770

Gergen, K. J. & Gergen, M. (2004). *Social construction: entering the dialogue.* Taos Institute Publications.

Gergen, K. J. (2014). From mirroring to world-making: research as future-forming. *Journal for the theory of social behaviour,* 45 (3), 287-310. DOI: https://doi.org/10.1111/jtsb.12075.

Gergen, K. J. (2015). *An invitation to social construction.* SAGE Publications.

Gergen, K. J. (2021). *The relational imperative: resources for a world on edge.* Focus Book: Taos Institute Publications.

Gersick, C. J. G. (2016). Adventures in qualitative analysis. In Elsbach, K. D. & Kramer, R. M. (Eds.), *Handbook of qualitative organizational research: innovative pathways and methods* (pp. 311–317). Routledge.

Goffman, E. (1974). *Frame Analysis: an essay on the organization of experience.* Harper & Row.

Gottlieb, M., Wagner, E., Wagner, A., & Chan, T. M. (2017). Applying design thinking principles to curricular development in medical education. *AEM education and training,* 1(1), 21–26. DOI: https://doi.org/10.1002/aet2.10003.

Gray, D., Brown, S., & Macanufo, J. (2010). *Gamestorming: a playbook for innovators, rulebreakers and changemakers.* O'Reilly & Associates.

Kimbell, L. (2011). Rethinking designing thinking: part I. *Design and culture,* 3(3), 285–306. https://doi.org/10.2752/175470811x13071166525216.

Kolko, J. (2015). Design thinking comes of age. *Harvard business review,* 66-71. Retrieved 28 June 2022, from https://hbr.org/2015/09/design-thinking-comes-of-age.

Kuhn, T. (1962). *The structure of scientific revolutions.* University of Chicago Press.

Leavy, P. (2020). *Method meets art, third edition: arts-based research practice.* Guilford Publications.

Lindberg, T., Noweski, C. & Meinel, C. (2010). Evolving discourses on design thinking: How design cognition inspires meta-disciplinary creative collaboration. *Technoetic arts,* 8 (1), 31-37. DOI: https://doi.org/10.1386/tear.8.1.31/1.

Lugmayr, A. (2011). Applying "design thinking" as a method for teaching in media education. In *Association for computing machinery,* 332–334. DOI: https://doi.org/10.1145/2181037.2181100.

Luka, I. (2019). Design thinking in pedagogy: framework and uses. *European journal of education, research, development and policy,* 54 (4), 499-512. DOI: https://doi.org/10.1111/ejed.12367.

McNamee, S. (1988). Accepting research as social intervention: implications of a systemic epistemology. *Communication quarterly,* 36, 50-68. DOI: https://doi.org/10.1080/01463378809369707.

McNamee, S. (2010). Research as social construction: transformative inquiry. *Health and social change,* 1(1), 9-19. Retrieved 30 june 2022, from https://mypages.unh.edu/sheilamcnamee/publications/research-social-construction-transformative-inquiry.

McNamee, S. (2014). Research as relational practice: exploring modes of inquiry. In G. Simon & A. Chard (Eds.), *Systemic inquiry: innovations in reflexive practice research,* (pp. 74-94). Everything is Connected Press.

McNamee, S. (2015). Ethics as discursive potential. *The Australian and New Zealand journal of family therapy,* 36, 419-433. DOI: https://doi.org/10.1002/anzf.1125.

McNamee, S. & Gergen, K.J. (1999). *Relational responsibility: resources for sustainable dialogue.* SAGE Publications.

McNamee, S. & Hosking, D.M. (2012). *Research and social change: a relational constructionist approach.* Routledge.

Melles, G., Howard, Z., & Thompson-Whiteside, S. (2012). Teaching design thinking: expanding horizons in design education. *Procedia - social and behavioral sciences,* 31, 162-166. DOI: https://doi.org/10.1016/j.sbspro.2011.12.035.

Montuori, A. & Donnelly, G. (2020). *Creativity and the future. In Runco, M., & Pritzker, S. Encyclopedia of creativity* (3rd. ed., pp. 250-257). Elsevier Science.

Nijs, D. (2019). *Advanced imagineering: designing innovation as collective creation.* Edward Elgar Publishing Limited.

Performatory. (n.d.). *Performatory.* Retrieved 30 June 2022, from https://www.performatory.nl/.

Plattner, H., Meinel, C.; Leifer, L. (2016). *Design thinking research: making design thinking foundational.* Springer Cham.

Pickering, A. (2013). Being in an environment: a performative perspective. *Natures sciences sociétés,* 21, 77-83. DOI: https://doi.org/10.1051/nss/2013067.

Pickering, A. (2022). *Improvisation and agency: comparing domains of improvisation seminar,* Conference, Columbia University (non published material).

Ponterotto, J. G. (2006). Brief Note on the Origins, Evolution, and Meaning of the Qualitative Research Concept Thick Description. *The Qualitative Report,* 11(3), 538-549. https://doi.org/10.46743/2160-3715/2006.1666

Rooijackers, M., Camargo-Borges, C., Marée, G., Weber, J., Brink, H. (2016). *Toolkit for design research & interventions.* Breda University of Applied Sciences. Retrieved 28 June 2022, from https://buas.libguides.com/designresearch.

Seelig, T. (2013). *Shift your lens: the power of re-framing problems.* Stanford technology ventures program. Retrieved 30 June 2022, from https://stvp.stanford.edu/blog/shift-your-lens-the-power-of-re-framing-problems.

Selvini, M. P., Boscolo, L., Cecchin, G., & Prata, G. (1980). Hypothesizing-circularity-neutrality: three guidelines for the conductor of the session. *Family process,* 19(1), 3–12. DOI: https://doi.org/10.1111/j.1545-5300.1980.00003.

Schnitman, D. F. (2010). Procesos generativos en el diálogo: complejidad, emergencia y auto-organización. *Plumilla Educativa,* 7(1), 61-73. DOI: https://doi.org/10.30554/plumillaedu.7.533.2010.

Terry, G., Hayfield, N., Clarke, V., & Braun, V. (2017). Thematic analysis. In Willig, C. & Stainton Rogers, W. (Eds.), *The SAGE handbook of qualitative research in psychology* (pp. 17-37). SAGE Publications.

Tomm, K. (1985). Circular interviewing: a multifaceted clinical tool. In Campbell D. & Draper R., *Applications of systemic family therapy: the Milan approach.* Grune & Station.

Tuyl, van G. (2009). *From engineer to co-creative catalyst: an inclusional and transformational journey.* University of Bath.

van Dam, A. (2019). E-nabling: how to enable co-creation. In Nijs D. (Ed.), *Advanced imagineering: designing innovation as collective creation* (pp. 151-166). Edward Elgar Publishing Limited. DOI: https://doi.org/10.4337/9781788976244.00021

van Dam, A. & Ouwens, F. (2016). *Let's get ACTIVE.* Breda University of Applied Sciences (internal publications).

Villar-Guhl, C. F. (2014). El consultor organizacional como arquitecto de posibilidades: transitando entre el construccionismo social y el pensamiento de diseño. *Sistemas familiares y otros sistemas humanos ASIBA,* 30(1), 80-100. Retrieved 28 June 2022, from https://asiba.org/index.php/asiba/article/view/22/21.

Whitney, S., & Trosten-Bloom, A. (2010). *The power of appreciative inquiry* (2nd ed.). Berrett-Koehler.

Wittgenstein, L. (1953). *Philosophical investigations.* (3rd ed. G. E. M. Anscombe, Trans.). Macmillan.

Authors
and
Illustrator

Celiane Camargo-Borges, Ph.D.

Lecturer and Researcher at Breda University of Applied Sciences, The Netherlands; Ph.D. supervisor at Canterbury Christ Church University, England; Faculty and member of the Taos Institute Board of Directors, USA; Visiting professor and guest lecturer at several universities around the world such as University of São Paulo in Brazil, Federal University of Rio de Janeiro in Brazil, University College Aspira in Croatia, University of Padova in Italy, among others. Working with constructionist theory and the design thinking approach, she is also the founder of Designing Conversations (designingconversations.us) where she consults on dialogue processes and Constructionist - Design Research. She is author of several articles and contributor to a variety of Handbooks such as The Sage Handbook of Social Constructionist Practice (Sage Publications); The Handbook of Arts-Based Research (Guilford Press); and The Handbook for Creative Futures (Taylor & Francis/Routledge).

Sheila McNamee, Ph.D.

Professor Emerita of Communication at the University of New Hampshire and co-founder and Vice President of the Taos Institute (taosinstitute.net). Her work is focused on dialogic transformation within a variety of social and institutional contexts including psychotherapy, education, healthcare, organizations, and communities. She is author of several books and articles, including Practicing Therapy as Social Construction (with E. Rasera & P. Martins, Sage Publications), Research and Social Change: A Relational Constructionist Approach (with D. M. Hosking, Routledge), Relational Responsibility: Resources for Sustainable Dialogue (with K. Gergen, Sage), and Education as Social Construction: Contributions to Theory, Research, and Practice (co-edited with T. Dragonas, K. Gergen, E. Tseliou, Taos WorldShare). Professor McNamee has written extensively about alternative visions of social research.